Elite • 158

African American Troops in World War II

Alexander Bielakowski • Illustrated by Raffaele Ruggeri

Consultant editor Martin Windrow

First published in Great Britain in 2007 by Osprey Publishing,
Midland House, West Way, Botley, Oxford OX2 0PH, UK
443 Park Avenue South, New York, NY 10016, USA

E-mail: info@ospreypublishing.com

ISBN: 978 1 84603 072 7

Editor: Martin Windrow
Page layouts by Ken Vail Graphic Design, Cambridge, UK
Typeset in Helvetica Neue and ITC New Baskerville
Index by Glyn Sutcliffe
Originated by PPS Grasmere, Leeds, UK
Printed in China through World Print Ltd.

07 08 09 10 11   10 9 8 7 6 5 4 3 2 1

A CIP catalog record for this book
is available from the British Library

FOR A CATALOG OF ALL BOOKS PUBLISHED BY OSPREY MILITARY AND
AVIATION PLEASE CONTACT:

NORTH AMERICA
Osprey Direct, c/o Random House Distribution Center, 400 Hahn Road,
Westminster, MD 21157
E-mail: info@ospreydirect.com

ALL OTHER REGIONS
Osprey Direct UK, P.O. Box 140 Wellingborough, Northants, NN8 2FA, UK
E-mail: info@ospreydirect.co.uk

Buy online at **www.ospreypublishing.com**

Artist's note

Readers may care to note that the original paintings from
which the colour plates in this book were prepared are
available for private sale. All reproduction copyright
whatsoever is retained by the Publishers. All inquiries
should be addressed to:

Raffaele Ruggeri,
Via Indipendensa 22,
40121 Bologna,
Italy
e-mail: raffaeleruggeri@libero.it

The Publishers regret that they can enter into no
correspondence upon this matter.

TITLE PAGE **May 1944: African American soldiers of the
25th Infantry Regiment (Colored), 93rd Division, advance
cautiously through thick bamboo jungle off the Numa-Numa
Trail on Bougainville, Solomon Islands. (NARA)**

AFRICAN AMERICAN TROOPS IN WORLD WAR II

INTRODUCTION

DURING World War II, hundreds of thousands of African Americans served in segregated units in the US military. The racial policies of the armed forces in the 1940s relegated most of them to tasks that were often both more physically demanding and more demeaning than those assigned to European Americans. Although each branch of the military had different policies regarding the admittance and employment of African Americans, the end of World War II found black Americans serving in every branch and in every theater of the war. Within the obvious limitations of space in a

Private Lloyd A. Taylor, an Army Air Corps dispatcher at Mitchel Field, NY City, posed with a Chinese-language primer. The caption states that this former medical student at Temple University studied languages as a hobby, and had already mastered Latin, Greek, Spanish, French, German and Japanese. Although an extreme case, Taylor's current employment is a stark reminder of the potential wasted by the Army's racial prejudices in the 1940s. (NARA)

August 1943: Undersecretary of War Robert P.Patterson is seen after inspecting the 369th Coast Artillery Regt in Hawaii, congratulating the regimental commander, Col Chauncey M.Hooper. Also shown are (second left) the commander of the Hawaiian Dept, LtGen Robert C.Richardson Jr, and (right) the 369th's regimental executive officer, LtCol Harry B.Reubel. (NARA)

book of this size, it is the author's hope to give at least a brief overview of the subject, together with basic facts on a few significant units.

While the majority of the approximately half-million African Americans who served overseas during World War II were draftees, overall they demonstrated the same enthusiasm (or lack thereof) for military service as their white counterparts.[1] For many African Americans their service in World War II was filled with irony: they were being asked to fight fascism and racism abroad, while they themselves endured racism at home. While the purpose of the two ugly signs was very different, it remains true that the world's justified outrage at the painting of the word *"Jude"* on German Jewish storefronts in the 1930s did not carry over to the use of the word "Colored" on public amenities in the American South.

The Selective Service Act of 1940 allowed for the induction of a number of African Americans equal to their percentage of the national population, which translated into 10.6 percent. However, since the majority of African Americans were generally ranked in the lowest two intelligence classes, the military resisted inducting that predetermined percentage.[2] The Army argued that if 10.6 percent of all draftees were African American, it would have to organize ten of its combat divisions completely with African Americans. The question of what to do with "excess" African Americans was a perpetual problem for the US military during the war.

---

[1] After December 1942, President Franklin D.Roosevelt ordered that the US military would no longer accept volunteers, and all American men were thereafter subject to Selective Service – conscription, commonly known as the "draft." Roosevelt's decision was made because too many men with important civilian skills were volunteering for combat duty, thus denying those skills to the national economy. Under the terms of the draft men with strategic skills would be deferred from service for the duration of the war.

[2] All incoming servicemen and women were tested and placed in five classes, Class I being the highest and Class V the lowest. The low ranking of African Americans was mainly a result of the poor quality of the education open to them in the South, where the majority of black Americans still lived.

While President Franklin D.Roosevelt favored desegregation of the military, he was prevented from acting upon his wish because the Democratic Party, his political power base, was considered a Southern party. If all of the Southern legislators withdrew their support from President Roosevelt he would find it impossible to pass any legislation. Instead, on June 25, 1941, Roosevelt signed Executive Order 8802, which prevented discrimination on the basis of race, creed, color or national origin by any corporation possessing a defense contract with the US government. Despite protests from business owners and labor unions, too much money was at stake for them to risk the government's wrath by non-compliance; for their part, the Southern legislators were generally unaffected by Executive Order 8802, because so little industry was located in their region.

US ARMY

The majority of the US military's segregated units were found in the Army, and African Americans were represented in every one of the Army's combat, support and service arms, including the Army Air Corps (later, Air Force). Despite their unequal treatment, it was in the Army that black Americans found opportunities for leadership unparalleled in the rest of American society at that time. Many African Americans reached senior leadership positions, and one officer reached the rank of brigadier-general. This achievement was all the more striking in that the pre-war US Army had fewer than 5,000 African Americans in just four regiments (24th & 25th Infantry and 9th & 10th Cavalry).

The most senior African American in the Army at the outbreak of World War II was **Benjamin O.Davis Sr.** Born in 1880, Davis began his military career as a second lieutenant in the Separate Battalion (Colored), District of Columbia National Guard in April 1898. Only two months later, he was offered the position of first lieutenant in the 8th US Volunteer Infantry (Colored). After serving with the 8th Volunteers until March 1899, Davis enlisted in the ranks of the 9th US Cavalry Regiment (Colored), and was promoted to corporal while serving as a clerk. He then passed a competitive examination for a Regular Army commission, and was sworn in as a second lieutenant in May 1901.

Over the next 40 years Davis rose to the rank of colonel, and rotated between duties as the Professor of Military Science and Tactics at Wilberforce University in Ohio and the Tuskegee Institute in Alabama; tours as the US military attaché in Monrovia, Liberia; and relatively brief periods of command with the 369th Infantry Regiment (Colored), New York National Guard, and the 372nd Infantry Regiment (Colored), Ohio National Guard. (Note: hereafter in this text, for the sake of brevity, the suffix "Colored" borne by all African American units will usually be omitted.) Since the Army was determined to prevent Benjamin Davis from commanding white officers, his skills were underutilized, and he seldom served in positions that befitted his rank and experience. During World War I, for instance, he was sent to the Philippines, where he served as the black 9th US Cavalry Regiment's supply officer. On this blighted career path Davis was following in the weary footsteps – from West Point, via the 9th Cavalry to Wilberforce, the Philippines and Liberia – of Col

September 1941: African American Army Air Corps cadets report in to Capt Benjamin O.Davis Jr, the commandant of cadets at Tuskegee Field, Alabama. Davis was only the fourth African American to graduate from the US Military Academy at West Point, NY, and was the first black American to be rated as a pilot in the Air Corps – see Plate A1. (NARA)

Charles D.Young (1865–1922), the third black American to graduate from West Point, with the class of 1889.

Finally, in January 1941, Davis became the first African American general officer in American history, when he was promoted to brigadier-general and ordered to Fort Riley, Kansas, to take command of the 4th Cavalry Brigade in the 2nd Cavalry Division. After serving for a total of 42 years and reaching mandatory retirement age, Davis was surprised to be called back to active duty, to serve as an advisor on "negro problems" in the US Army's Office of the Inspector General. He retired on July 14, 1948, after 50 years of active duty. Despite his achievements, Davis's career clearly demonstrated many of the worst consequences of racial prejudice in the US Army. African Americans were welcome – provided that they remembered their pre-ordained place in the power structure. The spectacle of an African American in officer's uniform violated all of the preconceived notions of those days regarding intelligence and leadership abilities, qualities of which white Americans were raised to believe they had a monopoly.

US Army Air Corps/ Force

The African Americans who served in the Army Air Force have probably received more attention than any other black American servicemen in World War II. The "Tuskegee Airmen" were seen as the most important "experiment" involving African Americans during the war, because these pilots were commissioned officers.[3] While the Army had much experience with black enlisted men, there were very few African American officers (only five achieved officer rank in the Regular Army between 1865 and 1939), and many senior Army officers did not believe that African Americans had the necessary intellectual and leadership capabilities to serve in commissioned rank. The success of the "Tuskegee Airmen" was a major blow to these racist assumptions.

The first African American officer to be accepted for pilot training was **Benjamin O.Davis Jr.** The future general's son was also the first African American admitted to the US Military Academy at West Point during the 20th century. Entering West Point in 1932, Davis endured four years of "silencing", during which no other cadet spoke to him unless required to do so in the classroom or on duty (an ordeal which Charles Young had also suffered half a century before). In 1936, Davis graduated near the top of a class that included the future general officers William P.Yarborough, Creighton W.Abrams Jr and William C.Westmoreland.

Davis had requested duty with the Air Corps, but he was informed that, since there were no "colored" units in that Corps, and the Army did not anticipate creating any, there was no need for a "colored" pilot. Instead, Davis was commissioned in the infantry and assigned to the 24th Infantry Regiment at Fort Benning, Georgia. After a year with the 24th Infantry and another year as a student at the Infantry School, he became the Professor of Military Science and Tactics at the Tuskegee Institute. Reflecting on his father's Army career, Davis accepted this assignment with a sense of doom, believing that he could also look forward only to years rotating between Wilberforce University and Tuskegee. Thankfully, after being promoted to general rank, Benjamin O.Davis Sr. requested his son be assigned as an aide, and the younger officer moved to Fort Riley, Kansas.

After only a few months at Fort Riley, Davis found out that the Army was reversing its policy on African Americans in the Air Corps. Davis was among the first class of 13 black aviation cadets at the Tuskegee Army Air Field. After completing flight training, Davis was quickly promoted to lieutenant-colonel and made the commander of the newly formed **99th Pursuit Squadron (Colored)** – the first African American unit in the Air Corps.

All members of the black Air Corps units organized during World War II had to overcome racial prejudice on several levels. Initially, there were no African American instructors available for flight or other training, and white instructors generally tended to demand higher standards of black students than they did from other Americans. An example of this attitude is the fact that only five of the first 13 African American aviation cadets completed the program, which was a significantly higher failure rate than encountered among white cadets. Even after an African American training cadre had been established, black aviation cadets had to endure segregated facilities that were certainly "separate" but far from "equal." The officers' club at the Tuskegee Army Air Field refused to admit African Americans, but there was no corresponding African American officers' club. Following the creation of the Army Air Forces in July 1941, all Army aviation-related

---

[3] The nickname came from their training site at Moton Field (later, Tuskegee Army Air Field) on the campus of the Tuskegee Institute (now Tuskegee University) near Montgomery, Alabama.

issues came under the direction of Gen Henry H. "Hap" Arnold. Like the rest of the AAF, Arnold considered African American pilots to be an "experiment," and felt no need to deviate from established Army rules regarding their segregation and treatment.

Even before the 99th Pursuit Squadron (later renamed the 99th Fighter Squadron) completed its training and left for combat duty in the Mediterranean, the **332nd Fighter Group** – which ultimately included the 99th, 100th, 301st and 302nd Fighter Squadrons – was organized to accommodate the further training of African American aviation cadets. Unfortunately, the influx of officers, cadets and enlisted men caused Tuskegee Field to become hopelessly overcrowded, a situation that was only slightly eased by the departure overseas of the 99th. The attitude of the surrounding white community did nothing to help the situation at the airfield. The "Jim Crow" system which reigned throughout the South in those days was very much alive in Tuskegee; this caused great resentment among the African American officers, many of whom were from the North and had never before experienced such overt racism.

Another problem that contributed to the cramped facilities at Tuskegee was an excess of non-flying personnel. Early in 1942, since the nation was now at war, the Air Corps stopped discharging individuals who had flunked out of flying school; instead, these men were retained at Tuskegee, despite having no suitable employment.

Members of a ground crew of the 332nd FG in Italy fit a drop tank to the wing of a P-51D Mustang. Left to right: Tech Sgt Charles K.Haynes, Staff Sgt James A.Sheppard, and Master Sgt Frank Bradley. The fighter group used auxiliary fuel tanks for long-distance flights while escorting bombers over German territory. (NARA)

Unlike failed white officer candidates, who were reassigned to other aviation programs, there was no other place for African Americans. By September 1943 the majority of the 286 failed officer candidates were still at Tuskegee, and suffering from very low morale. By the end of that October, Tuskegee reported an excess of 90 officers, most of whom were second lieutenants. By then, an average of seven African American officer candidate school graduates were arriving each month for non-flying assignments at Tuskegee.

Into combat

Though the 99th Fighter Squadron entered combat in the Mediterranean theater in June 1943 as part of the 33rd Fighter Group, its missions tended to center on strafing and dive-bombing, since there were still serious doubts within the AAF hierarchy about the abilities of its pilots. Despite being assigned these support missions rather than those that entailed a high risk of aerial combat, the 99th still had to put up with criticism for a lack of aggressiveness, insufficient air discipline, and not operating as a team. In September 1943, LtCol Davis was recalled from Sicily to assume command of the 332nd Fighter Group. At the same time he had to defend the 99th against the allegations that had been lodged by its superiors in the 33rd Fighter Group, who recommended that the squadron be relegated exclusively to coastal patrol duties.

This recommendation went up the chain of command and was endorsed by LtGen Carl Spaatz, the commander of Allied Air Forces

After long missions over enemy territory fighters often returned to base with only a few minutes' worth of gas left in their tanks; the officers' club of the 332nd FG was named "The Three Minute Egg Club" in honor of those pilots who got back just in time. Shown here are (left to right): 1st Lts Clarence A.Dart and Wilson D.Eagelson, and 2nd Lt William N.Olsbrook. Dart's service cap is a fine example of the "50-mission crush" beloved of AAF pilots. (NARA)

October 1944: Lt Andrew D.Marshall, a Mustang pilot in the 332nd Fighter Group with the 15th Air Force, was shot down by flak during a strafing mission over Greece. Greek partisans hid him from the Germans until the British III Corps invaded Greece a few days later. (NARA)

under Gen Dwight D.Eisenhower, and by Gen Arnold, the commander of the US Army Air Forces. However, before Gen George C.Marshall, Chief-of-Staff of the US Army, made a decision regarding the future of the 99th FS, he ordered the Army's G-3 (Operations) to carry out a study of the squadron's performance. Lieutenant-Colonel Davis defended his unit by pointing out that, because of segregation, the African Americans could not profit from the experience of white pilots. The men of the 99th were well trained and qualified, and could have become members of any squadron and functioned well in combat; however, segregation meant that they all started at the same level of inexperience. The final report of the G-3 found no qualitative difference between the 99th and white fighter squadrons assigned to the same theater and missions, and this effectively silenced the squadron's critics.

In January 1944 the 332nd Fighter Group as a whole deployed to Italy under the command of the newly promoted Col Benjamin O.Davis Jr. In July the 99th FS joined the 332nd, and the group ultimately participated in combat over Italy, Romania, the Balkans, France and Germany. It compiled an impressive combat record – flying more than 15,000 sorties, destroying more than 400 enemy aircraft, and never losing a bomber to enemy aircraft in more than 200 escort missions. Through their actions in combat these African American pilots earned the respect and acceptance of their white AAF counterparts.

The **477th Bombardment Group (Medium)** was the only other African American combat unit in the Army Air Force. Unfortunately, its officers and men never had the chance to prove themselves in combat, due to almost constant racial animosity.

The 477th – comprising the 616th through 619th Bombardment Squadrons – began its training at Selfridge Field, Michigan, but racial problems were created by the base commander, who prohibited African American officers from using the officers' club. The unit was then moved twice, first to Godman Field, Kentucky, and then to Freeman Field, Indiana, in an attempt to isolate them rather than to solve the racial problems. As a result of the Army Air Force's policy of segregation the 477th was plagued with both manpower surpluses and shortages. Three months after the group's original (and missed) deployment date, the 477th was short 26 pilots, 43 co-pilots, two bombardier-navigators and no fewer than 288 gunners. As a result, training took 15 months – five times the normal time – and the group was still not prepared for combat.

The racial climate in the group became increasingly volatile as whites tried to enforce segregation, and the result was a series of incidents at the Freeman Field officers' club. A total of 101 African American officers were arrested for attempting to enter the club against the orders of the base commander. The Army Chief-of-Staff, Gen Marshall, had to intervene personally, and ordered the release of the African American officers, who received only an administrative reprimand.

After the end of the war in Europe, Col Benjamin O.Davis Jr. and his African American officers replaced the entire white command structure of the 477th and of Godman Field, where the group had been transferred after the officers' club incident. Some African American officers argued that the segregationists had ultimately won, because the Army Air Force had thus created an all-black base. Nevertheless, African Americans did gain the opportunity to advance in rank and had command opportunities never before envisioned. The 477th BG was preparing for combat in the Pacific when the war ended.

On April 25, 1945, the same day that the US First Army met up with the Soviet Red Army at Torgau on the River Elbe, M5A1 Stuart tanks of the 761st Tank Bn park in the town square of Coburg, Germany; each tank battalion's Co D usually had these light tanks. The statue is of Prince Albert of Saxe-Coburg-Gotha, the consort of Queen Victoria. (NARA)

Armored Force and Tank Destroyers

While only a few African American tank units were organized, and though the tank destroyers were a short-lived branch of the Army, these units included African American officers, and proved that they could master complex machinery as easily as white Americans. Several tank destroyer units were manned exclusively by African Americans, from the commander down to the lowest private. The success of these units helped to prove that African American officers had leadership potential equal to that of whites.

The **761st Tank Battalion** was the first African American armored unit in combat. The battalion landed over Omaha Beach, Normandy, on October 10, 1944; it had six white and 30 African American officers, and 676 black enlisted men. From November 7, when it was committed to combat, the battalion spent 183 days in action; during this time the members of the 761st won 11 Silver Stars and 69 Bronze Stars.

On its first day in combat the lead tank of Company B was set on fire, the tank commander killed and another crewman severely wounded. A corporal from the crew manned a machine gun in the disabled tank, silencing several enemy machine gun positions and a German anti-tank team. The tank was hit twice more, but the crew remained with it. By the end of only their second day in combat, the 761st had certainly earned the right to their motto "Come Out Fighting."

During November the 761st Tank Bn suffered 24 killed in action, 81 wounded in action, 44 non-battle casualties, and 14 tanks lost. Tanks could be recovered and repaired, or replaced, but men were not so easy to come by. During November no replacements arrived, and the battalion ended the month with a shortage of 113 men. On December 4 the first replacements arrived, but these were not trained tankers and had to receive on-the-job training. Though African American soldiers anxious to see combat requested transfers to the 761st, the battalion remained perpetually short of trained personnel. During the Battle of the Bulge the battalion aided in the breakthrough to the surrounded 101st Airborne Division. By the end of the war in Europe the 761st was in Austria, where it met up with Soviet troops. The battalion remained in Germany until it was inactivated on June 1, 1946.

* * *

Not every tank and tank destroyer unit had the same leadership and motivation as the 761st Tank Battalion; and one of the worst examples of failure in these respects was the **827th Tank Destroyer Battalion**. The 827th TD Bn arrived in the European theater in November 1944 following a canceled deployment to the Pacific in spring 1944 – canceled because the battalion was deemed insufficiently trained. Just before the 827th departed for Europe the commanding and executive officers were replaced, in the belief that new leadership might improve the unit. All of the senior officers in the battalion shared the opinion that the unit would never perform adequately in combat and should be converted to a non-combat role or inactivated. By the time it was shipped to Europe the 827th had been on active duty for two years, during which time it had had eight different commanders, had been organized under four different tables of organization and equipment, and had been re-equipped with main weapons four times. This degree of turmoil would have been difficult for any unit, but it was worse for the 827th for other reasons.

Approximately 80 percent of the battalion's enlisted personnel ranked in the two lowest classes of the US Army's standardized intelligence tests. As a result, the battalion had never been able to form a strong cadre of noncoms, and the officers did not fare much better. African American junior officers were expected to motivate their men beyond any reasonable standard; when they "failed," they were removed and replaced with white officers, most of whom were either Southerners or had previously served with African American TD units that had been inactivated – and who therefore already had a negative attitude toward the future of the unit. Not surprisingly, these new white officers were no more successful in leading and motivating the 827th than their black predecessors. The commander then determined that the enlisted men, rather than the officers, were to blame for the unit's problems. In September 1944, as the unit prepared to move to Europe, preparations were disrupted by two court-martials, one involving an ax murder. Both cases indeed demonstrated the degree of indiscipline within the unit; neither officers nor NCOs were able to control their men.

After arriving in France the battalion performed a five-day march in December 1944 over icy roads to join the Seventh Army. So many accidents, breakdowns, cases of speeding and column-breaking, slow starts and late arrivals occurred that when the battalion arrived many of its vehicles immediately went in for significant repairs. It was an inauspicious beginning, and things would only get worse.

On December 20 the 827th was attached to the 12th Armored Division. The battalion was placed in reserve for three days, during which it saw no action but experienced problems with discipline among its crews, many of whom left their vehicles unguarded to gather firewood and build fires against the bitter cold. On January 6, 1945, the battalion was ordered to assist the 79th Infantry Division; but before the 827th could move out, an officer and an enlisted man shot each other when the officer attempted to break up a fight among the soldiers, and a disgruntled soldier attacked the first sergeant of another company. The sergeant, while shooting at his attacker, accidentally hit another innocent enlisted man. In yet another company, the company commander reported that approximately 75 percent of his men were missing.

March 28, 1945: correspondent Ted Stanford of the Pittsburgh *Courier* interviews 1st Sgt Morris O.Harris, a tanker of the 784th Tank Battalion. Here Harris is leaning on an M3 halftrack; each tank company had one halftrack in its maintenance section, and others were on the table of equipment of headquarters, recon and mortar platoons. Established in 1907, the Pittsburgh *Courier* was once the country's most widely read African American newspaper, with a national circulation of almost 200,000. (NARA)

Between January 8 and 20 the companies of the 827th performed at varying levels – some better than could possibly be expected, and others very poorly. In one incident, on January 14, a tank destroyer that was parked in a barn where anti-tank mines were stored caught fire. When ordered to drive the burning vehicle out before the mines exploded, the crew refused. Instead, white infantrymen ran into the barn and carried the mines out before the whole structure caught fire.

The 827th TD Bn's problems resulted in an investigation by the Inspector General's office, and this disclosed some instructive facts. Some companies of the 827th had acquitted themselves well, despite their own officers' low expectations; this was especially creditable when seen against the background – they were strafed by German aircraft, and fighting in support of white American infantrymen who were themselves disorganized and confused. Nevertheless, every white officer of the 827th expressed doubts about his men's abilities and courage. The Inspector General made three primary recommendations. These were, firstly, that the 827th be withdrawn from the line, given additional training, and then be returned to combat; secondly, that the men refusing to engage the enemy be tried by court-martial; and thirdly, that the commanding officer be replaced. The commanding general of VI Corps, to which the battalion was attached, recommended instead that the unit be disbanded, and his superior, the commanding general of Seventh Army, agreed.

However, the 6th Army Group did not concur. It seems that the investigating officer had questioned only the officers, and not the enlisted men of the 827th. A new investigating officer interviewed enlisted members of the battalion, and found that most of them were competent in their tasks, but that the overwhelming majority did not want to go back into combat. After the German surrender in May 1945 the issue of the 827th was finally settled when the battalion was named as a surplus unit so that it could be returned to the United States.

It is important to be clear about the reasons for the problems within the 827th. These were mostly the result of poor training, poor discipline, and poor leadership, exacerbated by frequent changes in organization, equipment, and officers. Nevertheless, parts of the battalion performed well enough that fair-minded officers concluded that more skillful leadership at crucial points in the battalion's life would have resulted in a far more effective unit.

Cavalry

More than 10,000 African American cavalrymen served during World War II. After the Army decided to dismount the horse cavalry, however, they were uncertain what to do with these troopers. On February 25, 1943, the 2nd Cavalry Division was activated with African American enlisted personnel.[4] Despite being trained as a combat division, and despite the need for more combat troops in Italy, after the 2nd Cavalry Division began arriving in Oran, Algeria, on March 9, 1944, it was inactivated and its personnel used to create support and service units. One small unit of African American cavalrymen retained their horses throughout the war,

---

[4] During World War II the 1st and 2nd Cavalry Divisions retained their pre-war "square" structure, each with two cavalry brigades of two regiments. The units of the 2nd Cav Div were 4th Cav Bde (9th & 10th Cav Regts), and 5th Cav Bde (27th & 28th Cav Regts). Meanwhile, all infantry divisions in the US Army adopted a "triangular" structure, which eliminated the brigades and included instead three infantry regiments, each of three battalions.

but they did so only in order to train white officer cadets at the US Military Academy. A small number of black cavalrymen traded their horses for armored cars and saw combat in Italy and the Pacific, as the division reconnaissance troops of the 92nd and 93rd Infantry Divisions.

Field, Coast and Antiaircraft Artillery

During World War II, African American soldiers were found in all three artillery branches in the US Army. The Army had distinguished between Field and Coast artillery since 1901. The differences between the two were self-evident: field artillery was mobile and employed on the battlefield, while coast artillery was generally immobile and designed to protect the American coast from invasion. Before World War II a new type of unit was created from within the Coast Artillery: Antiaircraft Artillery, whose importance was dramatically emphasized by events in Europe in 1939–40 and in the Pacific theater in 1941–42.

During World War II the Army organized 27 African American field artillery battalions. While 11 of these battalions were assigned to the African American 2nd Cavalry, 92nd and 93rd Infantry Divisions, and nine (including the three assigned to the 2nd Cavalry) were later reorganized as Engineer battalions, the remaining ten were organized as separate battalions generally coming under corps commands. These units were equipped with either 105mm or 155mm howitzers, and were attached at random to divisions in need of non-division artillery support assets.

At the outbreak of the war the Army had more "traditional" than AA coastal artillery units. By the end of the war, however, Coast Artillery functions had largely vanished as the reality of modern airpower became apparent. (The Coast Artillery also included additional searchlight and barrage balloon battalions, the latter to defend American troops and installations on the ground by preventing enemy low-altitude strafing runs.) As the war progressed, coast and AA artillery units within the USA increasingly became "caretakers" for stateside installations. Just as the war demonstrated that tanks were better than tank destroyers at killing

June 28, 1944: men of the 333rd Field Artillery Bn dig in one of their 155mm M1 howitzers soon after arriving in Normandy; each such battalion had three batteries each with four howitzers. This unit was one of ten non-divisional African American field artillery battalions to see combat as corps or army assets. The 155m howitzer could send a 95lb shell out to a maximum range of 9 miles. (NARA)

other tanks, so it also proved that aircraft were better than artillery at destroying other aircraft. This downgrading of their role led to a large number of coastal and AA units being manned by African American soldiers, who were generally not trusted by the Army hierarchy to perform more critical tasks. In turn, as manpower shortages became more apparent, African American Coast and AA Artillery units were often reorganized as Engineer and Quartermaster elements, in order to maintain the flow of supplies to combat units (see below, Support and Service Troops).

INFANTRY

The largest percentage of African American combat soldiers was found in the infantry, and more than 20,000 black infantrymen fought in Europe and the Pacific. Not only did many African Americans serve in segregated infantry units, but some were part of an experiment that involved the creation of the first racially integrated units in American military history. This experiment was so successful that it helped to justify President Harry S.Truman's decision to integrate the US military in 1948.

92nd Infantry Division

During World War I this formation had seen four months of combat on the Western Front, where it participated in the 1918 Meuse-Argonne offensive, and suffered more than 1,500 casualties. On October 15, 1942, the division was reactivated at Ft McClellan, Alabama, with the 365th, 370th and 371st Infantry Regiments, the 597th through 600th Field Artillery Battalions, and Engineer and Medical battalions both numbered 317th. The 370th Infantry was the first unit of the division to arrive in Italy, and went into combat on the Arno river front north of Rome on August 24, alongside the 1st Armored Division; the other division units went into action on October 6.

During the northern Italian campaign the 92nd "Buffalo" Division saw significant action, and suffered 2,997 battle casualties including 548 killed and 206 missing; only 56 men were listed as prisoners. It was reorganized in March/April 1945, when the 365th Infantry became a replacement training unit and the 371st was assigned rear security duties; for the last few weeks of the war it had one black regiment (370th), one white (473rd), and one "Nisei" Japanese American regiment (442nd Regimental Combat Team).

Though the 92nd Division represented less than 2 percent of African American troops in the Army, it received disproportionate media attention. This was not always from positive motives; the division's combat performance was mixed, and there were always those who were eager to slander African American GIs generally by seizing on particular incidents. As with so many other black units, the core of the problems

September 1943: the headquarters staff of the 92nd Inf Div established in an ancient Greek temple of Neptune in Italy. Sitting at the improvised desks are (front to back): Sgts James Shellman, Gilbert A.Terry, John W.Phoenix, Curtis A.Richardson and Leslie B.Wood. In front of the desks are (front to back): Tech Sgt Gordon A.Scott, Master Sgt Walter C.Jackson, Sgt David D.Jones and WO Carlyle M.Tucker. (NARA)

September 7, 1944: a combat patrol from the 92nd Inf Div advance, some 3 miles north of Lucca, Italy. The bazooka team have just fired an AT rocket; the M9A1 model bazooka had a maximum range of 300 yards. By this date each rifle company had five bazookas, and they were also issued on a generous scale to other battalion and regimental sub-units for antitank defense. (NARA)

November 1944: soldiers of an 81mm mortar platoon from the 92nd Inf Div in action against targets near Massa in northern Italy. The weapons company of each of the three battalions of each infantry regiment had six of these mortars. (NARA)

suffered by those of the 92nd Division was poor leadership (starting with the division commander, MajGen Edward M.Almond), and inadequate training. The white officers assigned to the formation were unhappy to be there; significant numbers of them were – deliberately – selected from among Southerners, many of whom proved unable to see beyond their ancestral prejudices.

93rd Infantry Division

The regiments of this formation had seen more combat in World War I than any other American units. It had been activated in December 1917, and organized from African American National Guard units from New York, Illinois, Connecticut, Maryland, Massachusetts, Ohio, Tennessee and the District of Columbia, and African American draftees from South Carolina. By the time of America's entry into the war the French Army had been fighting at hideous cost for three years; it was desperate for reinforcements and – with its own extensive colonial infantry component – was free of any neuroses about black combat troops. Consequently, the regiments of the 93rd were "loaned" to the French; it was originally intended that they would be returned and reorganized as a division of the American Expeditionary Force, but this did not happen. Instead, the regiments remained attached to French divisions until the end of the war in November 1918. They first went into action in the Verdun sector in June 1918, and went on to fight in the Champagne–Marne sector that fall; by the Armistice in November they had suffered more than 3,500 casualties and earned 322 gallantry decorations.

Reactivated on May 15, 1942, at Ft Huachuca, Arizona, the 93rd Division included the 25th, 368th and 369th Infantry Regiments, with the 593rd through 596th Field Artillery Battalions and the 318th Engineer and Medical battalions. The division was deployed to the Pacific, arriving on Guadalcanal progressively between January and March 1944. It served in New Guinea, the northern Solomons and the Bismarck Archipelago; however, owing to Army prejudice against African American units much of the division would spend the war performing labor and security duties. The 25th Infantry did see combat when it was attached to the "Americal" Division in March-April 1944 on Bougainville island. The 93rd Cavalry Reconnaissance Troop was also attached to XIV Corps to raid, patrol and maintain perimeter positions. In April 1945 the 93rd Division occupied Morotai, Dutch New Guinea, and recorded scattered skirmishes along the northwestern coast of the island, where the division continued its labor and security missions. Since the Army prevented the 93rd as a whole from seeing any significant combat, the division's wartime battle casualties amounted to only 138 men killed and wounded.

March–April 1944: soldiers of the 25th Inf Regt, then detached from its parent 93rd Inf Div to support the "Americal" Div, wait behind an M4A3 Sherman tank to assault Japanese positions along Empress Augusta Bay on Bougainville in the Solomon Islands. (NARA)

555th Parachute Infantry Battalion

This unit was born as a test company, activated at Fort Benning, Georgia, on December 30, 1943, as the 555th Parachute Infantry Company. The Army authorized the formation of a company with African American officers and enlisted men; all members of the company were to be volunteers, with an enlisted cadre selected from the 92nd Infantry Division. On November 25, 1944, after months of training, the company moved to Camp Mackall, North Carolina, where it was reorganized and redesignated as Company A of the 555th Parachute Infantry Battalion.

In May 1945, the 555th was sent to the West Coast of the United States to fight forest fires. Stationed at Pendleton Field, Oregon, the battalion's paratroopers participated in dangerous missions throughout the Pacific Northwest during the summer and fall of 1945. Nicknamed the "Triple Nickles" or the "Smoke Jumpers," the battalion returned to Camp Mackall in October 1945. The 555th then transferred to Fort Bragg, North Carolina, where it remained for the next two years and was attached to the 82nd Airborne Division. On December 15, 1947, the battalion was inactivated and most of its personnel were reassigned to the 3rd Bn, 505th Airborne Infantry Regiment.

April 1944, beside the East–West Trail, Bougainville: Sgt John C. Clark and Staff Sgt Ford M. Shaw, from Co E, 25th Infantry, clean their Garand rifles. The constant damp and filth of the jungle, and the M1's relatively complex semi-automatic action, made this a frequent and very necessary precaution. (NARA)

Volunteer infantry replacements

By December 1944 the US Army was experiencing severe shortages of infantry replacements in Europe. The shortfalls of riflemen began in July 1944, soon after the invasion of France. The problem was so severe that the Army began retraining enlisted men from other specialties to serve as infantry-men. The German Ardennes offensive of mid December further exacerbated the situation. The only readily available and relatively untapped source of manpower was the African American service and support units already serving in the European theater.

The suggestion of drawing upon these units for volunteer infantry replacements was welcomed by the Supreme Allied Commander, Gen Dwight D.Eisenhower; however, since integration was still un-acceptable to many senior officers and politicians, he had to find a way to hide his real intention. Therefore, a request was put out for volunteers from all service and support units, regardless of race; publicly, it was stated that if there were more black volunteers than were needed for existing African American combat units, those men would be used in other organizations.

The call for volunteers was issued on December 26, and since white units had already been combed out for infantry replacements, the overwhelming majority of

the volunteers came from among those for whom the appeal was originally intended – African Americans. Within two months almost 5,000 of them signed up, but since the Army could not afford to strip too many service and support units, the number accepted was initially limited to 2,500. As part of the arrangement the volunteers had to give up any rank they possessed in their previous units; thus, a first sergeant (the most senior NCO) in a Quartermaster unit would have to be willing to become a private in order to serve as an infantryman.

In January 1945 the first volunteers gathered for six weeks of infantry conversion training. After training, the African American infantrymen were organized into 53 platoons, each with a white platoon leader and platoon sergeant. The platoons were divided between two armored divisions (the 12th and 14th) and eight infantry divisions (the 1st, 2nd, 8th, 9th, 69th, 78th, 99th and 104th.) Each platoon included about 60 men – almost 50 percent more than the normal strength, in order to provide replacements for battle casualties. Three volunteer platoons were assigned to each division, one for each of its infantry regiments. At the end of the war it was made clear to the African American volunteers that the experiment had ended, and the majority of them were reassigned to African American units.

March 1944: a stick of 16 African American soldiers ride a C-47 transport on the way to one of their required five qualifying jumps before being awarded their "wings" at Fort Benning, Georgia. All ranks of the entire 555th Parachute Inf Bn would be African Americans; they would make dangerous jumps, but against forest fires in the Pacific Northwest rather than any human enemy. (NARA)

Crewed by African American GIs, US Army 2½ ton trucks and a Dodge weapons-carrier wind precariously along a mountainside on the Ledo Road, the only land supply route between Allied rear bases in India and troops in northern Burma and China. (NARA)

The experiment was carefully scrutinized by Eisenhower's headquarters. In July 1945, after the cessation of the war in Europe, a survey was undertaken among the white officers and platoon sergeants who had had contact with the African American platoons. In addition, an anonymous questionnaire was submitted to more than 1,000 white enlisted men to determine their attitudes toward the black riflemen. (Interestingly, no African Americans were interviewed.)

More than 80 percent of the white officers and NCOs interviewed believed that African American soldiers had performed "very well" in combat, and an almost equal number believed that African Americans could perform as well as white infantrymen if they had the same training and experience. Nearly all the white soldiers were surprised that, despite initial apprehension, the white and black infantrymen worked well together. The majority of the officers thought that the experiment should be continued and expanded, rather than retaining the segregated African American units.

Recommendations based on these findings were opposed by many senior Army officers, including the Army Chief-of-Staff Gen George C.Marshall and Gen Omar N.Bradley, the senior American field commander in Europe. Bradley argued that most of the African American platoons had participated in only minor combat operations; that they were made up of African Americans of "above average" intelligence; and that racial tension had arisen when the "integrated" companies were in rest and recreational areas. Marshall agreed with Bradley regarding the unusual quality of the volunteers and the uniqueness of the emergency that had prompted their employment. (It should be noted that both Marshall and Bradley, while professional Army officers of the highest caliber, haled from Southern states – Virginia and Missouri, respectively.)

Nevertheless, the volunteer platoons exploded many racial myths – and first, that of African American cowardice. If that were true, then why were thousands of black soldiers willing to trade the safety of duties in the rear – and many of them, their NCO pay and status – for combat in the snowy forests of the Bulge, against German units that had recently proved so aggressive? Secondly the myth that close contact between the races would result in conflict; in fact, there were very few racial incidents in the "integrated" companies. The last myth to be exposed was the belief that Southern officers were better suited to lead African American units, because of their experience of contact in civilian life. Since the placement of the volunteer platoons was not dependent on preconceived segregationist notions, platoon leaders and company commanders had been chosen fairly randomly, and included many Northern officers. The success of the volunteer platoons could therefore have little to do with the regional background of the officers.

In the end, the most long-term effect of the lessons of the volunteer platoons in the Battle of the Bulge would not be felt until July 26, 1948, when President Harry S.Truman signed Executive Order 9981, which provided equal treatment and opportunity for all members of the US military regardless of race.

Drivers from the 666th QM Truck Co, who chalked up 20,000 miles each without an accident since arriving in the ETO. Soldiers like these were instrumental in successfully supplying the US Army via the Red Ball Express. Left to right: Tech 5 Sherman Hughes, Tech 5 Hudson Murphy and Pfc Zacariah Gibbs. Note that all have acquired the M1944 "Ike" jacket. (NARA)

Support and service troops

By far the largest number of African Americans in the US Army served in support and service units. Every one of the Army's support and service support arms contained African American soldiers, who were frequently called upon to perform hazardous and crucially important duties with little or no recognition for their efforts. The majority of these duties were physically demanding, and some were considered beneath the dignity of white soldiers.

Many African American units were converted to new designations or specializations when they arrived overseas. In most cases they performed tasks for which they had never been specifically trained. The African American units in greatest demand and most consistently employed were those of the Engineer and Quartermaster branches of the service. While it might be imagined that such troops would require a fair amount of specialized training, they generally needed nothing more than physical strength and the ability to operate a motor vehicle. Although the first units shipped were generally less well trained than those that followed, the sense of urgency early in America's participation in the war put a higher value on simply filling immediate needs.

These units, who received little attention or fame, were in fact often among the first to arrive in combat zones. For instance, black engineers arrived before other American ground units at Port Moresby, New Guinea, the most vital single bastion of resistance to the Japanese operations there. Right across the immense expanses of the Pacific, they arrived just behind initial landing forces in order to construct airfields, and the roads and anchorages necessary to keep a steady stream of supplies moving forward to the troops on the front lines. Equipped with bulldozers, trucks, or simply on foot, they moved across the icy wilderness of Alaska, the jungles and hills of the China–Burma–India theater and the coral reefs of the Pacific, building the infrastructure necessary for the military transportation without which combat operations were simply impossible.

African American Port and Amphibious Truck companies found themselves attached to Army and Marine units for the invasions of Pacific islands such as Saipan, Tinian, Iwo Jima and Okinawa. During the battle of Iwo Jima, beginning on February 19, 1945, two US Army Port companies and three Amphibious Truck companies (equipped with DUKWs) were attached to V Amphibious Corps (Marine). Port companies manned harbours throughout the world, even in places where no port had ever before existed. In Normandy on June 6, 1944, the African American 320th AA Balloon Bn set up barrage balloons to protect the invasion fleet and the troops on the beaches from low-flying German aircraft. At the same time, Amphibious Truck, Quartermaster and Ammunition companies began unloading and transporting the supplies without which the beachhead could not have been established and defended.

African American Transportation companies were attached to infantry and armored divisions as they fought their way eastwards across Europe. Many of these companies became semi-permanent elements of these divisions, even serving as temporary infantrymen when circumstances required. For instance, during the drive across France the 57th Ordnance Ammunition Co was engaged by 65 Germans at the

French town of Peronne, with no other American units in support. The soldiers of the company killed 50 and captured the remaining 15 Germans; four men were cited for bravery during this encounter, and were awarded two French Croix de Guerre, one Silver Star and one Bronze Star.

The logistic lifeline of the advancing armies was, notoriously, stretched out perilously long and thin during the many months that the original Normandy beachhead remained the only available disembarkation point. This lifeline depended upon the Quartermaster truckers, who sped supplies forward along the roads of NW Europe by the priority traffic system christened the "Red Ball Express." In the end, the sheer quantity of work performed by African American units was more than planners had ever envisioned before the war. Many of these small units changed their designations and functions as needed; some of them – such as the dump truck companies – were always in demand. In total, more than 4,000 small African American service and support units were organized during World War II.

In March 1944, before the invasion of France, the majority of the nearly 700,000 African American soldiers were still in the United States; but by December 1944 more than two-thirds of them were overseas. The trend continued, and by April 1945 this figure

Private William A. Reynolds displays a machine gun bullet which lodged above the windshield of his ambulance when he was strafed by a German plane near the front in France. He wore the spent bullet on his dog-tag chain for good luck. (NARA)

had risen above 70 percent. Of the approximately 470,000 black soldiers serving overseas in December 1944, around 170,000 were Quartermaster troops, 110,000 were Engineers, and 65,000 were Transportation troops.

For the most part the Quartermaster truck and service companies, the laundry and dump truck companies, and the Engineer and Port units spent their overseas service in harbors, base camps and depots; they performed routine duties, with few if any opportunities for heroism. Though their service was in the main rather unexciting, they were no more or less efficient than similar units of any race. Interactions between African American and white soldiers, and between black American troops and foreign civilians, were generally more often positive than negative. The efficiency of most African American units was never as high as it could have been if the training and leadership they were given had truly been equal to that of white units; but likewise, their efficiency was generally never as poor as white segregationists continually claimed.

Life overseas
The American Red Cross created a number of clubs staffed with and exclusively for African Americans. By February 1944 there were 23 African American clubs, but the very existence of the segregated clubs smacked of the "separate, but equal" treatment that so many black Americans were forced to endure in the Southern USA. The American Red Cross and its clubs were independent of the federal government; but the close association between them and the Army overseas did not permit the average enlisted man or officer to notice any clear distinction between the two institutions or their policies.

Of the letters written by white American soldiers who mentioned the issue of race, the majority discuss their surprise at the lack of racial prejudice among the British people. They were shocked that many British women saw no problem in dancing with or even dating African American soldiers (some believed that black Americans somehow convinced the allegedly gullible British that they were Native Americans). Others took consolation from the belief that only the British lower classes were friendly to African Americans. While this issue might seem unimportant (other than to white Americans trying to get a date), some were concerned as to how the friendly treatment African Americans generally received in Britain might affect their post-war expectations when they returned home. While the post-World War I saying had been, "How do you keep them down on the farm after they've seen Paris?", white soldiers now seemed to worry, "How can you keep them in their place now that they've dated a British woman?"

For African American soldiers the color-blindness of the British Isles was an unexpected pleasure; but for white officers, the situation in Britain was complicated. Officers serving with African Americans were both relieved that they did not have to worry about racial animus among their hosts, and concerned as to how white GIs would react to the relaxed British attitudes. White officers serving with white American soldiers tended to share their men's opinions – that this exposure to British calmness over race was simply going to make things more difficult in post-war America.

US NAVY

Prior to World War II, African American sailors were only allowed to serve in Navy kitchens. The US Navy's senior leadership initially resisted extending their role beyond kitchen duties; eventually, however, two warships were crewed exclusively with African American sailors, though they were commanded by white officers. No black officers were available for these ships, because only 13 African Americans were commissioned as line officers in the Navy during World War II. Additionally, the US Navy organized several African American construction battalions, which saw combat in the Pacific.

India, July 1943: African Americans off duty in crisp khakis, enjoying a rickshaw ride. For all the demeaning treatment they often endured, the war did bring nearly half a million black Americans an opportunity to see far countries and other cultures – some of which gave them food for thought. (NARA)

Steward's Mate Doris Miller

Doris Miller, known as "Dorie" to his friends, was born in Waco, TX, on October 12, 1919. In high school he was a fullback on the football team, and he worked on his father's farm. On September 16, 1939, the 20-year-old Miller enlisted in the US Navy as a mess attendant, 3rd class. He joined the Navy instead of the Army because he wanted to travel, to learn a trade (cooking), and to earn money to help his family. Miller's first assignment was aboard the USS *Pyro* (AE-1), an ammunition ship. On January 2, 1940, he transferred to the battleship USS *West Virginia* (BB-48), where he became the ship's heavyweight boxing champion.

On December 7, 1941, Miller was aboard the *West Virginia* when the Japanese attacked Pearl Harbor. Having risen at 6.00am that morning,

Miller was collecting laundry when general quarters was sounded. He headed for his battle station, an antiaircraft battery magazine, only to find it already destroyed by a torpedo strike. Miller then went up to the main deck, where he began carrying wounded sailors to safety. Then an officer ordered him to the bridge of the ship to aid the already wounded captain; and after doing this, Miller manned a .50cal AA machine gun, firing on the Japanese aircraft until he ran out of ammunition, and the order was put out to abandon ship.

During the attack the *West Virginia* was struck by two armor-piercing bombs (both of which penetrated the ship's deck), and five torpedoes in her left side. The explosions from those strikes caused severe flooding below decks, and she slowly sank to the bottom of "Battleship Row." Unlike the most famous battleship in Pearl Harbor that morning, the USS *Arizona* (BB-39), the *West Virginia*'s losses were quite moderate: only 130 killed and 52 wounded out of a crew of 1,541 men. For his bravery that morning, Miller was awarded the Navy Cross, the Navy's second highest award for valor after the Medal of Honor.

Miller was next assigned to the armored cruiser USS *Indianapolis* (CA-35) and, in spring 1943, to the newly constructed escort carrier USS *Liscome Bay* (CVE-56). During Operation "Galvanic" on November 20–23, 1943 – the assault landings on Makin and Tarawa atolls in the Gilbert Islands – the *Liscome Bay*'s aircraft supported operations ashore. At 5.10am on November 24 a torpedo from the Japanese submarine *I-175* struck near the stern of the carrier. The aircraft bomb magazine detonated

soon afterwards; the carrier sank within minutes, and Dorie Miller was among the 646 sailors who lost their lives. On June 30, 1973, the Navy commissioned the USS *Miller* (FF-1091), a Knox-class frigate, in his honor. For African Americans, Dorie Miller was the first and greatest hero of World War II.

USS *Mason* (DE 529)

The destroyer escort USS *Mason* was one of only two US Navy vessels whose crews were composed entirely of African Americans. Just as the 99th Fighter Squadron had been an "experiment" for the AAF, so the *Mason* was considered an experiment to find out whether African Americans were capable of performing more than menial tasks in the Navy. The captain of the *Mason*, LtCdr William M.Blackford, had previously captained the USS *Phoebe*, a minesweeper working in the Aleutian Islands. Blackford, who came on active duty from the Naval Reserve in January 1941, was only two semesters short of finishing a PhD in chemistry at the University of Virginia. His great-grandmother, Mary Berkeley Minor Blackford, had been noted as an abolitionist, but he himself was no crusader for African American rights; he simply treated his sailors as human beings.

May 27, 1942: Adm Chester W.Nimitz, C-in-C Pacific Fleet, pins the Navy Cross – the US Navy's second highest medal for valor after the Medal of Honor – on Steward's Mate 3rd Class "Dorie" Miller at a ceremony in Pearl Harbor, Hawaii – the scene of Miller's acts of bravery aboard the stricken battleship USS *West Virginia* during the attack of December 7, 1941. On November 24, 1943, Miller would be lost at sea when the carrier USS *Liscome Bay* was torpedoed by a Japanese submarine. (NARA)

The first real test for the USS *Mason* was her shakedown cruise in April 1944, during which both the machinery of the ship and the crew's ability to work with their new equipment were tested. Exercises, both day and night, included towing, refueling, gunnery and dropping depth charges. The *Mason* and her crew performed well during the cruise, but the Navy's Bureau of Personnel report included more discussion of the ship's appearance than of her actual performance.

The USS *Mason*'s second voyage, to the United Kingdom, would also be her most difficult. As part of Convoy NY-119 the destroyer endured 30 days of near-record wind and waves, which sank three tugs, eight car floats and five cargo barges. On October 18, 1944, when land was sighted and the month-long ordeal was almost at an end, the weather got even worse: the wind increased to 60 knots and visibility dropped to zero. Unfortunately, this proved to be more than the *Mason*'s structure could endure, and the ship's deck split – two beams in one compartment collapsed, and the seam holding the deck together broke.

On June 2, 1942, William Baldwin
became the first African American
US Navy recruit classified for
General Service – prior to this
date they could only join the Navy
as stewards, working in the ships'
kitchens. (NARA)

Nevertheless, within two hours the deck was repaired. The *Mason* then
assisted 12 other ships in the convoy, before sailing to the coast of
France to salvage barges until the end of that month.

Commander Blackford recommended his crew for a unit
commendation for their efforts during Convoy NY-119, but the
commendation never materialized. The convoy's commander also
recommended the *Mason* and her captain for decorations; again, they
were never awarded. Amazingly, the *Mason*'s crew did not know about
these nominations until 50 years later, when a researcher produced a
book on the ship.

During their several combat cruises the crew of the USS *Mason*
experienced different attitudes regarding their race in the different
ports they visited. The reception they received while visiting Belfast,
Northern Ireland, was the most positive; from the Ulster point of view
the destroyer's crew were simply another bunch of "Yanks." While the
English had often referred to them, amiably enough, as "Tan Yankees"
(an un-English term they must have learned from Americans), the
Northern Irish made no distinction whatever, and they were well treated
during their stay.

On June 12, 1945, Blackford was abruptly promoted and transferred
to the Great Lakes Naval Training Station. The ship's next captain,
LtCdr Norman Meyer, had a very different attitude toward the men of
the USS *Mason*. He wrongly believed that the majority of his crew were

illiterate, and that he had inherited a ship with a poor record. Meyer, a US Naval Academy graduate, was responsible for the most embarrassing incident involving the *Mason* when he accidentally rammed the USS *Spangenburg* while pulling into a North River pier in New York City. After only three months aboard Meyer relinquished command; and the *Mason* was decommissioned a month later, in October 1945.

In 1998 the Secretary of the Navy, John H.Dalton, decided to name an Arleigh Burke-class destroyer the USS *Mason* (DDG 87), to mark the contributions of the sailors of the wartime DE 529.

PC 1264

The patrol craft PC 1264 was the second of the two US Navy vessels whose crews were composed entirely of African Americans. Though she was actually in service longer than the *Mason*, the PC 1264 – a smaller vessel, with a smaller crew (only 300 tons as opposed to the *Mason*'s 1,100, and 63 men against the destroyer's 156) – has sunk into even greater obscurity than her counterpart.

Popularly known as "subchasers," the 369 patrol craft launched during World War II were almost exclusively crewed by reservists and draftees with minimal sea experience. Their duties were wide-ranging, and included escorting convoys, hunting submarines, sinking small enemy vessels, shooting down aircraft, bombarding landing areas, and leading landing craft in to invasion beaches. Designed to be produced easily in small yards, the subchasers were used in all theaters of the war.

March 20, 1944: at the Boston Navy Yard, African American sailors look over their newly commissioned ship, the USS *Mason* (Destroyer Escort 529) – the first Navy vessel to have a predominantly African American crew. (NARA)

A gun crew of six African Americans who received the Navy Cross for standing by their 40mm AA gun when their ship was damaged by enemy attack in the Philippines. Left to right: Steward's Mates Jonell Copeland, Que Gant, Harold Clark Jr, James E.Dockery, Alonzo A.Swann and Eli Benjamin. (NARA)

The captain of PC 1264, Lt Eric Purdon, was not chosen because of any particular qualities relating to his African American crew. Rather, he seems to have been selected simply because he was available and had served on another subchaser, before briefly – for three months – commanding yet another. Purdon was given the chance to volunteer for the assignment and did so willingly; it brought him two things he wanted – a command, and a challenge. All of the other ship's officers were also volunteers. With one exception (the executive officer, who was a jazz aficionado and had black friends), none of the other officers had any particular feeling for or against African Americans. It is interesting to note that all of them were Northerners or Californians.

The PC 1264 was commissioned on April 24, 1944, at the Brooklyn Navy Yard. The ship's 22 months of service proved to be largely uneventful; she spent her career patrolling the east coast of the United States and the Caribbean. The closest she came to combat was during stops in Southern ports, when the officers and crew were threatened with lynchings, for being "race-mixers" or "bothering our women," respectively.

In May 1945 a momentous event occurred on the PC 1264 when a new officer reported aboard: Ensign Samuel L.Gravely Jr., who would become, in 1971, the first African American admiral in the US Navy. The ship was preparing for duty in the Pacific when the war ended on August 15, 1945. After VJ-Day many officers and sailors began to be discharged; Lt Purdon turned over command of PC 1264 on October 31. By the time the ship was decommissioned on February 7, 1946, the entire ship's complement was only five officers and 28 sailors.

(continued on page 41)

US ARMY AIR FORCE
1: LtCol Benjamin O.Davis Jr. 99th FS; Sicily, August 1943
2: Captain, 477th BG; USA, 1944
3: Technical Sergeant

A

ARMOR & ARTILLERY UNITS; NW EUROPE, WINTER 1944–45
1: Staff sergeant, Field Artillery
2: Corporal, Tank Destroyer Force
3: Major, 761st Tank Bn

B

CAVALRY, 1943–44
1: First sergeant, 2nd Cavalry Division
2: BrigGen Benjamin O.Davis Sr. 2nd Cavalry Division
3: Second lieutenant "Jackie" Robinson

C

INFANTRY, 1944–45
1: Pfc, 555th Parachute Inf Bn; Camp Mackall, NC, 1945
2: 1st Lt Vernon J.Baker, 370th Inf Regt, 92nd Inf Div; Italy, 1945
3: Private, 370th Inf Regt; Italy, August 1944

D

E

SUPPORT & SERVICE TROOPS
1: M/Sgt, 6888th Postal Directory Bn, Women's Army Corps; Uk, 1945
2: Tech 4, Corps of Engineers; Italy, 1945
3: Sgt, Military Police, 92nd Inf Div; Italy, 1945

F

1

2

3

G

US MARINE CORPS
1: Gny Sgt Gilbert H.Johnson; Montford Point Camp, NC, 1945
2: Sergeant, "utilities"
3: Pfc, "dress blues"

Naval Construction Battalions

In October 1942 the US Navy created the first segregated construction battalions (CBs, better known as "Seabees"). Eventually the Navy established 17 Special and two regular Construction Battalions with white officers and African American sailors, and more than 14,000 black Americans served in these segregated units during World War II. Men assigned to these construction battalions received instruction in a wide variety of duties, some involving particular skills and others merely requiring physical strength. Additionally, since most of their work took place close to the front lines, they also received small arms and other combat training.

The construction battalions performed all of the Navy's overseas construction work, including building airfields, roads, housing, defensive positions, docks, wharves, bridges, canals and storage facilities, and also unloaded equipment. Seabees were also frequently called upon to fight alongside ground combat troops or to protect themselves from Japanese attacks. For example, in the Palau Islands, 200 African American Seabees joined an assault against Japanese positions, and half of them became casualties during the first week of combat. The Seabees' efforts made the difference between victory and defeat during a number of Pacific island operations.

December 1942: men of the US Navy's 34th Construction Bn disembark from a landing craft during assault training. While "Seabees" were specifically tasked with construction work, they were also expected to defend themselves and their sites from Japanese attacks. (NARA)

The Port Chicago disaster, July 17, 1944

As the war in the Pacific expanded, Port Chicago, California, located 35 miles north of San Francisco, became a major munitions facility for the US Navy. By 1944 expansion and improvement of the pier at Port Chicago allowed for the loading of two ships simultaneously. Most of the dangerous work, the loading and unloading of munitions, was done by African American sailors. Unfortunately, neither the sailors nor their white officers had received any special training in the loading and unloading of munitions, though they did receive some instruction in general cargo handling. The majority of their experience came from working with the munitions on a day-to-day basis. The loading of ships went on around the clock, and the different work crews developed a sense of competition regarding who could load the most in an eight-hour shift. Since this race helped to increase the speed of loading, officers encouraged what they saw as healthy rivalry.

On the evening of July 17, 1944, two merchant ships were being loaded at the Port Chicago pier, the SS *Quinault Victory* and the SS *E.A.Bryan*. The munitions being loaded were a combination of high explosive and incendiary bombs, depth charges and ammunition – more than 4,000 tons in all. In addition, 16 railroad cars were on the pier carrying another 400 tons of munitions. There were 320 cargo handlers, crewmen and sailors performing the stevedore duties that night.

In September 1944, during the 1st Marine Div's bitterly resisted invasion of Peleliu in the Palau Islands, this group of African American Seabees acted as stretcher bearers for the 7th Marines. (NARA)

At 10.18pm an enormous explosion ripped into the night sky; a column of smoke and flames erupted from the pier, and just six seconds later a second massive explosion followed aboard the *E.A.Bryan*. The seismic shock wave was so massive that it was felt as far away as Boulder City, Nevada. The *E.A.Bryan*, the pier and nearby buildings completely disintegrated; the *Quinault Victory* was spun into the air, its remains crashing back into the bay 500 feet from its anchorage. The 320 men on duty that night were killed instantly, while another 390 were wounded, and the blast damaged every building in Port Chicago. The air filled with splinters of glass and other debris, later found as far as two miles away. The blast even caused damage 48 miles away across the Bay in San Francisco. Of the 320 men killed in the explosion 202 were African Americans; the disaster at Port Chicago accounted for 15 percent of all African Americans killed in World War II.

Despite the devastation, less than a month after the worst home-front disaster of World War II, Port Chicago was again loading munitions bound for the Pacific. The repercussions of the explosion were both positive and negative. Prior to the disaster, US Coast Guard instructions on safe ship loading were often violated, because it was felt that they were either not safe enough or not fast enough; the officers and men on the pier experimented with new procedures which they felt were both safer and faster. After the explosion, the Navy instituted a number of

Enlisted sailors serving on Espiritu Santo Island in the New Hebrides, placing 6in shells in magazines at the Naval Ammunition Depot; they wear working "dungarees." Left to right: Seamen 1st Class Dodson B.Samples, Raymond Wynn, Edward L.Clavo and Jesse Davis. (NARA)

changes in munitions handling procedure, and formalized training with certification was required before a loader was allowed on the docks. The munitions themselves were also redesigned to make them safer while loading.

The explosion had obviously shaken everybody working in the port. For the African Americans, working in a segregated unit under dangerous conditions, discontent soon gave way to open hostility. On August 9, 1944, less than a month after the explosion, African American survivors of the disaster were ordered to begin loading munitions at the Mare Island facility; subsequently 258 black sailors refused to continue to load munitions. Of these, 208 were given summary court-martials and were sentenced to bad conduct discharges and the forfeit of three months' pay for disobeying orders. The remaining 50 were given general court-martials on the charge of mutiny. Since the United States was at war, these men were eligible for the death penalty; in the event they each received sentences of between eight and 15 years at hard labor. In January 1946 all of them were given clemency and the remainder of their sentences were remitted. It was not until December 23, 1999, that President William J.Clinton granted them a full and complete pardon.

Beginning on June 1, 1942, for the first time in history, the US Marine Corps began to enlist African Americans; the first of more than 19,000 to serve during the war was Pvt Howard P.Perry, seen here in the forest-green service uniform with service cap. (NARA)

US MARINE CORPS

The outbreak of World War II found the US Marine Corps without a single African American officer or enlisted man. In fact, the Marine Corps had never allowed African Americans to join, and was the last branch of the US military to admit them when it was ordered to do so by President Roosevelt in June 1942. Under these circumstances it should not be surprising that not a single African American Marine Corps officer was commissioned during World War II.[5] Despite these limitations, many African American units were formed by the Corps, and saw active service in the Pacific.

Although the Marine Corps began to allow African Americans to enlist, few were interested, since the Corps was commonly known as the "white man's service." In the first month of recruiting only 63 African Americans enlisted, and four months produced only half of the 1,200 that the Marine

[5] The first African American Marine officer was commissioned on November 10, 1945 – Frederick C.Branch, a veteran of the 51st Defense Bn, was commissioned second lieutenant in the USMC Reserve, but soon thereafer was discharged from active duty.

Corps believed they needed as a minimum cadre for the proper training of the roughly 1,000 African American troops who would enter the Corps each month as a result of the Selective Service system, beginning in January 1943.

The Commandant of the Marine Corps, LtGen Thomas Holcomb, made it clear that the Corps did not want African Americans even though it was now forced to accept them. In March 1943, Holcomb issued Letter of Instruction 421, which remained classified until after World War II. This document stated that African Americans would never be placed in a situation in which they were superior in rank to any white Marine. The Corps did not want this situation to be obvious to African Americans, so they also had a policy of removing white NCOs from African American units as soon as competent black NCOs were prepared to replace them.

Segregation in the Marine Corps began with the training of African American draftees, which took place at a newly established cantonment in the grounds of Camp Lejeune, North Carolina – Montford Point Camp. The commander of Montford Point Camp was Col Samuel A. Woods Jr, a Southerner who had graduated from the Military College of South Carolina (better known as the Citadel). He accepted the idea of segregation, but his calmness and fairness nevertheless earned him the respect of his troops. Woods cultivated a paternalistic relationship with his Marines, and there was some wry affection in his nickname of "the Great White Father."

The battle of Saipan in June 1944 saw the first African American Marines killed and wounded in combat, when men of support companies got drawn into infantry fighting. Here Staff Sgt Timerlate Kirven (left) and Cpl Samuel J.Love Sr., uniformed in khakis, are posed for the photographer wearing their Purple Hearts. (NARA)

Since the Marine Corps needed competent African American non-commissioned officers, they relied upon black recruits who had previous military experience with the Army or Navy. One of the first of these was **Gilbert H."Hashmark" Johnson**, who earned his nickname from wearing on his uniform sleeve three of the diagonal "hashmark" stripes indicating previous completed military enlistments. Born in 1905, Johnson joined the US Army in 1923 and served two enlistments with the 25th Infantry Regiment. Starting in 1933, he also served an enlistment as a steward in the Navy; in May 1941 he rejoined the Navy, again as a steward, before being allowed to transfer to the Marine Corps in November 1942.

Since Johnson had infantry experience ranging from company clerk to squad leader, he was ideally suited to serve in the Corps. After completing basic training he was chosen as an assistant drill instructor under a white NCO, and after his subsequent promotion he became a drill instructor. In January 1945, Gunnery Sergeant Johnson became the sergeant-major of the Montford Point Camp. He continued to serve in the USMC after World War II, retiring in 1955. Two years after his death in 1972, the Marine Corps renamed Montford Point Camp as Camp Gilbert H.Johnson.

51st Defense Battalion

The first, and for a time the only African American Marine Corps combat unit was 51st Defense Battalion (Composite). Defense battalions were organized to solve the problems faced by the Marine Corps in placing garrisons on the smaller overseas possessions that the Navy used as bases, and in defending the naval bases that enabled the United States to project its power toward Japan. The most famous of the wartime battalions was a detachment from the 1st Defense Bn that fought at Wake Island.

By the end of 1942 the nature of the defense battalions' role was changing. Rather than repulsing amphibious landings, they were more likely to be defending against Japanese air strikes. In June 1943 the term "Composite" was removed from the 51st Defense Bn, and the unit was reorganized. The battalion now contained three groups: a Seacoast Artillery Group, equipped with 155mm guns; an Antiaircraft Artillery Group, with 90mm guns; and a Special

Weapons Group, equipped with machine guns, 20mm and 40mm automatic cannon.

In January 1944 the 51st Defense Bn began its journey to the Pacific when it moved by rail to San Diego, CA; it was assigned to replace the 7th Defense Bn, already located in the Ellice Islands, and set sail aboard the merchantman SS *Meteor* on February 11. The 51st Defense Bn remained on Nanoumea and Funafuti in the Ellice Islands for roughly six months, during which it saw almost no enemy action. While in the Ellice Islands the battalion had reorganized as an AA unit, losing its 155mm guns but adding more 90mm, and exchanging its machine guns and 20mm cannon for more 40mm weapons. On September 8, 1944, the battalion sailed for Eniwetok Atoll in the Marshall Islands, which was under sporadic surveillance and occasional harassment by Japanese aircraft. Duty on Eniwetok was routine and relatively boring, enlivened only by the occasional crash or forced landing of American planes. The battalion sailed back to America in November 1945, and disbanded at Montford Point in January 1946.

52nd Defense Battalion
On December 15, 1943, the second African American USMC defense battalion was organized from a cadre of 400 officers and men transferred from 51st Defense Bn before it left for the Pacific. On August 24, 1944, after more than six months of training, the 52nd moved to Camp Pendleton, California, and on September 21 boarded the transport USS *Winged Arrow* (AP-170). Arriving in the Marshall Islands, they took over the defense of two Marine air groups from other AA units on Majuro and Kwajalein atolls. For six months, from October 1944 to March 1945, the battalion guarded the Marine airstrips against Japanese air attack, and formed reconnaissance parties that searched the smaller islands for Japanese stragglers.

The 52nd Defense Bn deployed to the recaptured island of Guam on May 4, 1945, remaining there for the rest of the war. In November 1945 the 52nd relieved the 51st on Kwajalein and Eniwetok. In May 1946, after returning to Montford Point, the battalion was re-designated the 3rd Antiaircraft Artillery Bn (Composite).

Seen here on April 17, 1945, Pfc Luther Woodward of the US Marine Corps' 4th Ammunition Co was awarded the Bronze Star for "his bravery, initiative and battle-cunning." The award would later be upgraded to the Silver Star. (NARA)

Other Marine Corps units

By the spring of 1943 the Marine Corps discovered a need for stevedores to move supplies from the rear areas into combat zones. The Corps organized two kinds of units – Depot companies and Ammunition companies – to fill this need. Although these companies were envisioned as merely a source of labor, while the two defense battalions were seen as combat units, the reality proved quite the opposite. The defense battalions spent most of the war fighting boredom, while the depot and ammunition companies saw combat on Saipan, Tinian, Guam, Peleliu, Iwo Jima and Okinawa, and suffered most of the African American Marine Corps casualties.

The 1st Marine Depot Co – the first of no fewer than 51 – was activated on March 8, 1943, and the 1st Marine Ammunition Co – the first of 11 – was formed on October 1 that year. In both types of company African American troops carried rifles, carbines or sub-machine guns, but were not equipped with any heavier weapons. On June 15, 1944, the depot companies saw their first action on Saipan when a squad fought as infantry to reinforce a thinly held line, and the majority of a company helped eliminate Japanese infiltrators. On Saipan, Private Kenneth J.Tibbs became the first African American in the Marine Corps to be killed in combat.

March 1945: three African American Marines pause to eat during the battle of Iwo Jima. Left to right: Pfcs Willie J.Kanody, Elif Hill and John Alexander. (NARA)

On September 15, 1944, the 1st Marine Division made an assault landing on the island of Peleliu, with the 11th Marine Depot Co and the 7th Marine Ammunition Co in support. The 11th Depot Co paid a price for their part in this battle, with 17 men wounded – the highest casualty rate of any African American USMC company during the war. The prolonged fighting for Okinawa involved approximately 2,000 African Americans, a larger concentration than for any previous battle. Black Marine casualties during the battle amounted to one killed and 18 wounded, one of them twice. By the end of the war 19,168 African Americans had served in the Marine Corps.

OTHER MARITIME SERVICES

US Coast Guard

The US Coast Guard traces its military roots to August 4, 1790, when Secretary of the Treasury Alexander Hamilton established the Revenue Cutter Service. The modern Coast Guard is a combination of five predecessors: the Revenue Cutter Service; the Lifesaving Service (created in 1878 and merged with the Revenue Cutter Service in 1915, the new service taking the name Coast Guard); the Lighthouse Service (created in 1789 and absorbed in 1939); and the Bureau of Navigation and Steamboat Inspection (itself a merger of two agencies organized in 1884 and 1838 respectively, absorbed in 1942).

While African Americans first began to serve in the Revenue Cutter Service in 1831, and 1st Lt Michael A.Healy became the first African American to command a US government vessel (the Revenue Cutter *Chandler*) in 1877, the Coast Guard itself did not accept African Americans to serve in capacities other than stewards until March 1942. The first group of 150 black volunteers was trained at Manhattan Beach Training Station, New York City; they received instruction in seamanship, knots, lifesaving and small-boat handling. While classes and other official activities were integrated, the sleeping and mess facilities remained segregated.

August 1944: Fireman 1st Class Charles Tyner, US Coast Guard, examines the considerable fragment hole in his helmet, received during the landings in Southern France – Operation "Dragoon." Tyner was lucky to escape with only a minor scratch. (NARA)

The majority of African Americans were assigned to shore duty, including security and labor details, and worked as yeomen, storekeepers, radiomen, pharmacists, coxswains, electricians, carpenters and boatswains. Other African Americans served on horse and dog patrols on America's beaches, on the watch for enemy infiltration.

Since so many African Americans were assigned to shore duty, the Coast Guard leadership had a legitimate manpower problem: it was nearly impossible to rotate white Coast Guardsmen to shore duties without transferring African Americans to cutters, which would have integrated the vessels. In June 1943, Lt Carlton Skinner proposed that a group of African Americans be integrated into the

Two US Coast Guard officers aboard a cutter on the North Atlantic patrol: Ens J.J.Jenkins (left) and Lt(jg) Clarence Samuels. (NARA)

crew of a single cutter as an experiment. The Commandant of the USCG, Adm Russell R. Waesche, agreed, and Skinner was promoted to lieutenant-commander and given command of the weather ship USS *Sea Cloud* (IX-99). The *Sea Cloud* had an integrated crew of 173 officers and men with four African American officers and 50 African American Coast Guardsmen.

Although the experiment of integration aboard the *Sea Cloud* lasted a year, no racial incidents occurred, and the integrated crew was just as efficient as any other in the Coast Guard. As a result the USCG began to integrate other cutters during the remainder of the war. More than 5,000 African Americans served in the Coast Guard during World War II, and about 965 rose to the ranks of petty or warrant officers. The first African American commissioned officer in the Coast Guard was Joseph Jenkins, who was commissioned as an ensign in the Coast Guard Reserve on April 14, 1943 – almost a full year before the first black Americans were commissioned in the Navy.

Of necessity, therefore, the Coast Guard became the first branch of the US military to desegregate. In fact, on July 26, 1948, when President Truman ordered the integration of the US military with Executive Order 9981, the Coast Guard was already desegregated.

The USCG were early to form integrated crews. Here two men, both from Ohio – John R. Smith (left) and Daniel J. Kaczorowski – operate their 20mm cannon aboard a Coast Guard-manned invasion transport during the Normandy landings. The original print shows the last spent shell casing still flying up as Smith slams the new magazine in place. (NARA)

February 8, 1943: the captain and some of the crew of the Liberty Ship SS *Booker T.Washington* pose for a picture just after completing their maiden voyage to England. Left to right: Second Mate C.Lastic, Midshipmen T.J.Young and E.B.Hlubik, Radio Operator C.Blackman, Chief Engineer T.A.Smith, Captain Hugh Mulzac, Chief Mate Adolphus Fokes, Lieutenant H.Kruley, Second Engineer E.P.Rutland, and Third Engineer H.E.Larson. (NARA)

US Merchant Marine

Merchant shipping has been an integral part of the American economy since before the founding of the United States. In fact, the impressment of American seamen by the British was the immediate cause of the War of 1812. During World War II the United States produced approximately 2,700 merchant ships, of which 17 were named for African Americans; the first of these, the SS *Booker T.Washington*, was christened in 1942.

Hugh Mulzac became the first African American member of the merchant marine to command an integrated crew during World War II, when for five years he served as the captain of the SS *Booker T.Washington*. Born on March 26, 1886, in the British West Indies, he became a seaman in his youth; he took US citizenship in 1918, and earned his captain's rating in the merchant marine that same year, but racial prejudice prevented his commanding a ship. More than 20 years passed before he was offered command of the *Booker T.Washington*, an integrated vessel whose crew represented 18 different nationalities. During World War II this ship made 22 voyages and carried 18,000 troops to Europe and the Pacific.

The US Maritime Service, the official training organization of the Merchant Marine, had a non-discrimination policy during a time when most of the US military was still segregated. Approximately 24,000 black Americans served as merchant seamen during World War II, which amounts to roughly 10 percent of the total. African Americans served in every capacity aboard these merchant ships, regularly going into combat zones to deliver men and supplies.

BIBLIOGRAPHY

Published primary sources:

Davis, Benjamin O., Jr., *Benjamin O. Davis, Jr.: American* (Washington, DC; Smithsonian Institution Press, 1991)

Gropman, Alan L., *Air Force Integrates, 1945–1964* (Washington, DC; Office of Air Force History, 1978)

Lee, Ulysses, *United States Army in World War II: Special Studies – Employment of African-American Troops* (Washington, DC; Government Printing Office, 1966)

MacGregor, Morris J., Jr., *Integration of the Armed Forces, 1940–1965* (Washington, DC; US Army Center for Military History, 1989)

Nalty, Bernard C., *Right to Fight: African-American Marines in World War II* (Washington, DC; Marine Corps Historical Center, 1995)

Osur, Alan M., *African-Americans in the Army Air Forces During World War II: The Problem of Race Relations* (Washington, DC; Office of Air Force History, 1977)

Shaw, Henry I., & Ralph W.Donnelly, *African-Americans in the Marine Corps* (Washington, DC; History and Museums Division, Headquarters Marine Corps, 1975)

Secondary sources:
General works

Alt, William E., & Betty L.Alt, *African-American Soldiers, European-American Wars: African-American Warriors from Antiquity to the Present* (Westport, CT; Praeger Publishers, 2002)

Astor, Gerald, *Right to Fight: A History of African-Americans in the Military* (Novato, CA; Presidio Press, 1998)

Brandt, Nat, *Harlem at War: The African-American Experience in WWII* (Syracuse, NY; Syracuse University Press, 1996)

Buckley, Gail L., *American Patriots: The Story of African-Americans in the Military from the Revolution to Desert Storm* (New York; Random House, 2001)

Canfield, Bruce N., *US Infantry Weapons of World War II* (Lincoln, RI; Andrew Mowbray Publishers, 1994)

Dabbs, Henry E., *African-American Brass: African-American Generals and Admirals in the Armed Forces of the United States* (Charlottesville, VA; Howell Press, 1997)

Edgerton, Robert B., *Hidden Heroism: African-American Soldiers in America's Wars* (Boulder, CO; Westview Press, 2001)

Hawkins, Walter L., *African American Generals and Flag Officers: Biographies of Over 120 African-Americans in the United States Military* (Jefferson, NC; McFarland, 1993)

Johnson, Jesse J., *Pictorial History of African-American Soldiers in the United States: In War and Peace (1619–1969)* (Hampton, VA: published by the author, 1970)

Lanning, Michael L., *African American Soldier: From Crispus Attucks to Colin Powell* (Secaucus, NJ; Carroll Publishing, 1997)

Kohn, Richard H., et al, *Exclusion of African-American Soldiers from the Medal of Honor in World War II: The Study Commissioned by the United States Army to Investigate Racial Bias in the Awarding of the Nation's Highest Military Decoration* (Jefferson, NC; McFarland & Company, 1997)

Kryder, Daniel, *Divided Arsenal: Race and the American State During World War II* (New York; Cambridge University Press, 2000)

Nalty, Bernard C., *Strength for the Fight: A History of African-American Americans in the Military* (New York; Free Press, 1986)

Nichols, Lee, *Breakthrough on the Color Front* (Colorado Springs, CO; Three Continents Press, 1993)

Wright, Kai, *Soldiers of Freedom: An Illustrated History of African Americans in the Armed Forces* (New York; African-American Dog & Leventhal Publishers, 2002)

US Army:

Abdul-Jabbar, Kareem, & Anthony Walton, *Brothers in Arms: The Epic Story of the 761st Tank Battalion, WWII's Forgotten Heroes* (New York; Broadway Books, 2004)

Arnold, Thomas S., *Buffalo Soldiers: The 92nd Infantry Division and Reinforcements in World War II, 1942–1945* (Manhattan, KS; Sunflower University Press, 1991)

Biggs, Bradley, *Triple Nickles: America's First All-African-American Paratroop Unit* (Hamden, CT; Archon Books, 1986)

Carter, Allene G., & Robert L.Allen, *Honoring Sergeant Carter: Redeeming an African-American World War II Hero's Legacy* (New York; Amistad Press, 2003)

The color guard, officers and men of the 41st Engineer Regt (General Service), at Ft Bragg, North Carolina. During the war the 41st Engineers served in Liberia, Algeria, Italy, France and Germany. (NARA)

Colley, David P., *Blood for Dignity: The Story of the First Integrated Combat Unit in the US Army* (New York; St Martin's Press, 2003)

Colley, David P., *Road to Victory: The Untold Story of World War II's Red Ball Express* (Washington, DC; Brassey's Inc, 2000)

Fletcher, Marvin E., *America's First African-American General: Benjamin O.Davis, Sr, 1880–1970* (Lawrence, KS; University Press of Kansas, 1989)

Gibran, Daniel K., *92nd Infantry Division and the Italian Campaign in World War II* (Jefferson, NC; McFarland & Company, 2001)

Goodman, Paul, *Fragment of Victory in Italy: The 92nd Infantry Division in World War II* (Nashville, TN; Battery Press, 1993)

Griggs, William E., *World War II African-American Regiment That Built the Alaska Military Highway: A Photographic History* (Jackson, MS; University Press of Mississippi, 2002)

Hargrove, Hondon B., *Buffalo Soldiers in Italy: African-Americans in World War II* (Jefferson, NC; McFarland & Company, 1985)

Knapp, George E., *Buffalo Soldiers at Fort Leavenworth in the 1930s and Early 1940s* (Fort Leavenworth, KS; Combat Studies Institute of the US Army Command & General Staff College, 1991)

McGuire, Phillip, ed., *Taps for a Jim Crow Army: Letters from African-American Soldiers in World War II* (University Press of Kentucky, 1993)

Moore, Brenda L., *To Serve My Country, To Serve My Race: The Story of the Only African American WACs Stationed Overseas During World War II* (New York; New York University Press, 1996)

Morehouse, Maggi M., *Fighting in the Jim Crow Army: African-American Men and Women Remember World War II* (Lanham, MD; Rowman & Littlefield, 2000)

Putney, Martha S., *When the Nation Was in Need: African-Americans in the Women's Army Corps During World War II* (Scarecrow Press, 2001)

Sasser, Charles W., *Patton's Panthers: The African-American 761st Tank Battalion in World War II* (New York; Pocket Books, 2004)

Stanton, Shelby L., *US Army Uniforms of World*

War II (Mechanicsburg, PA; Stackpole Books, 1991)

US Army Air Force:

Francis, Charles E., *Tuskegee Airmen: The Men Who Changed a Nation* (Boston; Branden Publishing Company, 1997)

Greene, Robert E., *Pictorial Tribute to the Tuskegee Airmen of World War II* (Fort Washington, MD; R.E.Green Publisher, 1992)

Holway, John B., *Red Tails, African-American Wings: The Men of America's African-American Air Force* (Las Cruces, NM; Yucca Tree Press, 1997)

Homan, Lynn M., & Thomas Reilly, *African-American Knights: The Story of the Tuskegee Airmen* (Gretna, LA; Pelican Publishing Company, 2001)

Homan, Lynn M., & Thomas Reilly, *Tuskegee Airmen* (Charleston, SC; Arcadia Publishing, 1998)

Jakeman, Robert J., *Divided Skies: Establishing Segregated Flight Training at Tuskegee, Alabama, 1934–1942* (Tuscaloosa, AL; University of Alabama Press, 1992)

McGee-Smith, Charlene E., *Tuskegee Airman: The Biography of Charles E.McGee – Air Force Fighter Combat Record Holder* (Boston; Branden Publishing Co, 1999)

McGovern, James R., *African-American Eagle: General Daniel 'Chappie' James, Jr* (Tuscaloosa, AL; University of Alabama Press, 1985)

Osur, Alan M., *Separate and Unequal: Race Relations in the Army Air Forces During World War II* (Washington, DC; Air Force History & Museums Program, 2000)

Phelps, J.Alfred, *Chappie: America's First African-American Four-Star General – The Life and Times of Daniel James, Jr* (Novato, CA; Presidio Press, 1991)

Sandler, Stanley, *Segregated Skies: All-African-American Combat Squadrons of World War II* (Washington, DC; Smithsonian Institute Press, 1998)

Warren, James C., *Freeman Field Mutiny* (San Rafael, CA; Donna Ewald Publishers, 1995)

US Marine Corps:

De Clouet, Fred, *First African-American Marines: Vanguard of a Legacy* (Nashville, TN; James C.Winston Publishing Company, 1995)

Fischer, Perry E., & Brooks E.Gray, *African-Americans and European-Americans – Together Through Hell: US Marines In World War II* (Turlock, CA; Millsmont Publishing, 1994)

US Navy:

Blackford, Mansel G., ed., *Board the USS Mason: The World War II Diary of James A.Dunn* (Columbus, OH; Ohio State University Press, 1996)

Kelly, Mary P., *Proudly We Served: The Men of the USS Mason* (Annapolis, MD; Naval Institute Press, 1995)

National Park Service, *Port Chicago Naval Magazine* (Washington, DC; Government Printing Office, 2005)

Newton, Adolph W., *Better Than Good: An African-American Sailor's War, 1943–1945* (Annapolis, MD; United States Naval Institute Press, 1999)

Purdon, Eric, *African-American Company: The Story of Subchaser 1264* (Annapolis, MD; United States Naval Institute Press, 2000)

Stillwell, Paul, ed., *Golden Thirteen: Recollections of the First African-American Naval Officers* (Annapolis, MD; Naval Institute Press, 1993)

PLATE COMMENTARIES

UNIFORMS

The uniforms worn by African Americans during World War II did not differ from those worn by their white counterparts. Since they are described and illustrated in much greater detail in other Osprey titles, only a brief summary will be repeated here.[6]

US Army

During World War II the "dress blues" uniform was not a required purchase item for Reserve, National Guard, or draftee officers or

---

[6] See Men-at-Arms 342, *The US Army in World War II (1) The Pacific*, 347 *(2) The Mediterranean*, and 350 *(3) Northwest Europe*. Also, Elite 46 & 51, *The US Army Air Force (1)* and *(2)*; Elite 59, *The US Marine Corps 1941–45*; and Elite 80, *The US Navy in World War II*.

enlisted men; due to wartime priorities and material shortages, even most newly commissioned Regular Army officers did not own one.

The World War II service uniform can be divided between winter and summer, as well as officer and enlisted models. The officers' winter dress consisted of a four-pocket wool service coat (tunic) with "peak lapel-collar" and integral cloth belt, of a dark "chocolate" shade of olive, and pale fawn trousers; this combination was generally referred to as "pinks and greens." Officers had the option of wearing a shirt of the same dark shade as the coat, or khaki; either shirt could be worn with a khaki or dark olive necktie. Late in the war, Gen Eisenhower popularized yet another type of coat, the M1944 wool field jacket or "Ike jacket." A waist-length garment modeled on the British battledress blouse, this was available for both officers and enlisted men, in "chocolate" or olive drab wool; it had been intended for field use, but was usually kept for service and walking-out uniform. Officers' summer service uniform consisted of a khaki shirt, trousers and necktie, with an optional khaki coat (without the cloth belt). Various overcoats, raincoats and mackinaws were available for bad weather.

The enlisted winter service uniform comprised an olive drab four-pocket coat with "notched lapel" collar (but without the integral cloth belt), and trousers; these came in both light and dark shades, but both appeared more yellow-brown than the officers' coat. The shirt was either khaki or a light shade of olive drab, and could be worn with either a khaki or a black necktie. A long, double-breasted wool overcoat and

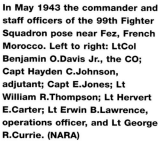

In May 1943 the commander and staff officers of the 99th Fighter Squadron pose near Fez, French Morocco. Left to right: LtCol Benjamin O.Davis Jr., the CO; Capt Hayden C.Johnson, adjutant; Capt E.Jones; Lt William R.Thompson; Lt Hervert E.Carter; Lt Erwin B.Lawrence, operations officer, and Lt George R.Currie. (NARA)

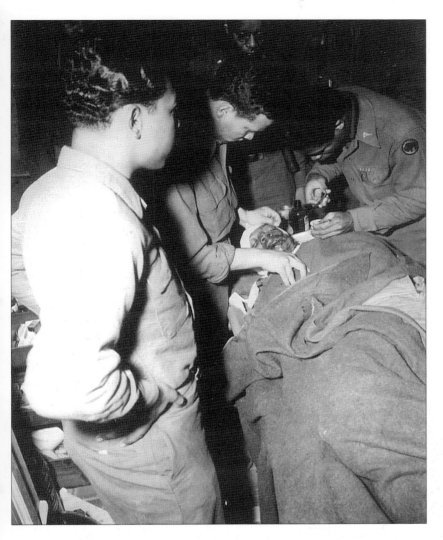

February 10, 1945, near Querceta, Italy: Capt Ezekia Smith, a company commander in the 370th Inf Regt, 92nd Div, receives treatment at the 317th Collecting Station after suffering shell fragments in his face and shoulders. Note the "Buffalo" shoulder sleeve insignia – see Plate D – and the Medical officer's cut-out caduceus badge on his left shirt collar. (NARA)

a rubberized raincoat were issued. The enlisted summer uniform was almost identical to the officers' model, and consisted of a khaki shirt, trousers and necktie, but lacked the khaki service coat.

When the United States entered World War II in December 1941 the service uniform and the combat uniform were basically identical apart from the addition of a steel helmet, leggings and web gear to the latter. Since the service uniform had not been designed specifically for field use it was impractical in that role: it lacked adequate pockets, was designed to be form-fitting rather than roomy, was hard to clean, and the necktie was as absurd in combat as the World War I "choker" collar had been. Beginning in 1941, a lined, hip-length, zip-fronted, windproof cotton poplin "Parsons" field jacket began to be issued. Herringbone twill fatigue jackets and trousers were also used for field wear, often in combination with pre-war wool or khaki uniform items.

The Army subsequently experimented with a completely new combat uniform, designed on the "layering" principle, that abandoned most of the older conventions. While this sateen cotton M1943 uniform, in the greenish "OD shade No.7," was not adopted in its entirety, parts of it did

March 21, 1944, Italy: Pvt Jonathan Hoag of the 92nd Div is decorated with the Croix de Guerre by Gen Alphonse Juin, commanding general of the French Expeditionary Corps, for courage while treating wounded even though he himself was wounded. Hoag wears the Fifth Army shoulder patch on his early pattern field jacket. (NARA)

find their way into general use. The most important item was the crotch-length M1943 field jacket, with four large pockets, epaulettes, and provision for attaching a pile liner and a hood.

Special field uniform items were issued for some types of troops, and acquired by others unofficially. The two most significantly different field uniforms were those specially designed for airborne and armored troops – respectively, the loose M1942 paratrooper uniform, with its many capacious pockets; and the heavily lined windcheater jacket with knit collar, cuffs and waistband, and bib-top overtrousers, produced to protect tank crews in winter.

A wide range of headgear was issued to American soldiers during the war, the most important of these being the service and garrison caps and the steel helmet. The service cap had a large round crown and a brown leather visor. Although it was the standard home service headgear, few wartime soldiers overseas would own one. The higher quality officers' model was popular among AAF flyers, who removed the crown stiffener supposedly for ease while wearing headphones – the consequent dashingly "crushed" appearance was probably of more importance. The garrison cap was modeled on the French *calot* sidecap of World War I, which could conveniently be folded flat while not in use. The garrison cap was available in khaki or the chocolate-like dark olive for officers, and in khaki or olive drab for enlisted ranks.

In 1941 most soldiers were still wearing the M1917A1 dishpan-style steel helmet modeled on that used by the British Army in World War I. The new pot-shaped M1 shell-and-liner design had been approved, but few had yet been manufactured; it was general issue by the end of 1942.

At the beginning of the war soldiers were issued the russet leather service shoe, which was roughly similar to a modern lace-up, ankle-length hiking boot. Over these, soldiers wore calf-to-instep cotton canvas leggings that laced through a number of eyelets up the outsides. These were unpopular – they soaked up water, chafed, and took too long to put on. Beginning in 1943 a much more sought-after "two-buckle" boot began to be issued, with a laced foot similar to the service shoe but with an integral leather gaiter-flap at the ankle, fastening with two buckled straps. Various specialist footwear was also available, including the paratroopers' high-lacing "jump" boots, and two types of canvas and rubber protective overboots for extreme winter conditions.

A: US ARMY AIR FORCE

A1: Lieutenant-Colonel Benjamin O.Davis Jr., 99th Fighter Squadron (Colored); Sicily, August 1943

At this time Col Davis was commanding officer of the 99th FS, then flying mainly ground-attack missions as part of 33rd Fighter Group. He wears the AN-H-15 summer flying helmet with goggles and oxygen mask/radio microphone, and the A4 summer flight suit under his leather A2 jacket and B3 lifejacket.

A2: Captain, 477th Bombardment Group (Medium) (Colored); USA, 1944

The heavier flight uniform worn for longer bomber missions in a roomier cockpit consists of the sheepskin B3 jacket and A3 trousers, and A6A boots. This B-25 pilot also wears the khaki summer version of the Army officer's service dress cap.

A3: Technical Sergeant

This ground crew NCO wears the ubiquitous one-piece herringbone twill (HBT) fatigue coverall, worn throughout the Army for dirty jobs around mechanical equipment, with his rank insignia inked on the sleeve; his headgear is the baseball-style B1 summer mechanic's cap.

B: ARMOR & ARTILLERY UNITS; NW EUROPE, WINTER 1944–45

B1: Staff sergeant, Field Artillery

This NCO wears a combination of casual cold-weather field dress items which would be equally common in the infantry. The M1 steel helmet was worn at most times and places where there was any danger of enemy artillery attack. The high-neck OD wool sweater has a low standing collar and five-button front; it is worn with standard issue wool pants in light shade OD, canvas leggings, and leather-soled russet field shoes. The only unusual feature is the rank insignia sewn to the sweater sleeves – not authorized on this garment, but typical of the latitude allowed by units in the front lines.

B2: Corporal, Tank Destroyer Force

This soldier has a camouflage net on his M1 helmet. His field jacket in light olive drab poplin is the "Parsons" type (often but erroneously called the M1941 – it had no such official designation); despite the introduction of the longer, greener-colored M1943 field jacket by late 1944 the original model was widely used until the end of the war. On the left sleeve he displays the shoulder sleeve insignia of the whole TD Force above his rank chevrons. His dark shade OD wool pants are tucked into "buckle boots" – the M1943 combat service boot, not yet widely available in the ETO and the object of much trading and larceny.

B3: Major, 761st Tank Battalion (Colored)

The steel shell of a large size M1 helmet is worn here – against sniper's bullets and shell fragments, always perilous to men in the open hatches of AFVs – over the top of the hard leather M1942 armored forces helmet, with its integral radio earphones; in this case the major's rank insignia is soldered to the helmet front.

The so-called tanker's jacket – actually the "winter field jacket" – bears the universal Armored Force shoulder insignia with the addition of the battalion number in black. To troops of other branches the comfortable, warmly lined jacket, with knit collar, cuffs and waistband, was probably the second most desirable type to acquire after the leather AAF flight jacket. It is worn here over the winter combat trousers; windproof, water-repellent, and fully lined with blanket material, these had high bib tops at front and rear. The shoulder holster rig for the M1911A1 .45cal semi-automatic pistol was more convenient in the tight confines of a tank turret than a conventional waist-belt holster.

C: CAVALRY, 1943–44

C1: First sergeant, 2nd Cavalry Division

This senior NCO wears the early-war service uniform of the remaining horsed cavalry units: the M1939 olive drab wool service coat, wool elastique breeches, OD wool shirt with khaki tie, and OD garrison cap with the yellow arm-of-service piping of the cavalry. On the right and left respectively of his notched-lapel collar he displays brass discs bearing the

August 19, 1945, in Rouen, France: Chaplain William T.Green, wearing captain's bars, conducts the wedding ceremony for Cpl William A.Johnson, 1696th Labor Supervision Co, and Pfc Florence A.Collins, 6888th Postal Directory Bn – note the shoulder patch of European Theater Advanced Base. This couple were the first African Americans to be married in the ETO. (NARA)

An African American MP staff sergeant at Fort Benning, GA, in April 1942. (NARA)

"U.S." cypher and the cavalry's crossed sabers. His chevrons and rockers of rank are worn on both sleeves, the divisional insignia on the left shoulder, and a slanting service stripe on the left forearm, marking a completed three-year enlistment. His russet riding boots are of non-regulation pattern and probably privately purchased.

C2: Brigadier-General Benjamin O.Davis Sr., 2nd Cavalry Division

The commanding general of the 4th Cav Bde also wears service uniform, but with the M1911 service hat, its black-and-gold cords and "acorns" indicating general officer's rank. His winter service coat in "chocolate" (OD shade No.51) wool elastique has the half-inch ring of contrasting OD shade No.53 mohair braid around the cuffs which was displayed by all officer ranks. The star of his individual rank, and the officers' cut-out "U.S." cyphers, are pinned to the epaulettes and both upper lapels respectively; he wears the 2nd Cavalry Division shoulder sleeve insignia, but not the cavalry-branch sabers on his lower lapels. General Davis' shirt is in the optional khaki shade No.1 cotton, worn with a black necktie. His riding breeches, in a contrasting light shade of drab, are worn with regulation elkhide legging-topped laced riding boots and spurs.

C3: Second lieutenant Jack Roosevelt Robinson

In 1947, "Jackie" Robinson would become famous as the first African American to play major league baseball, with the Los Angeles Dodgers; but he had already had his share of fame and controversy. He had been the first student at the University of California, Los Angeles, to receive a varsity letter in four different sports (baseball, basketball, football and track). In World War II he served originally as an enlisted man in the 761st Tank Bn, but, based on his educational achievements, he attended Officer Candidate School and was commissioned second lieutenant. However, Robinson did not ship out to Europe with his battalion – because he was court-martialed for refusing to sit at the back of a public bus in the area traditionally reserved for "coloreds". After being acquitted, he accepted an honorable discharge, and began playing professional baseball with the Kansas City Monarchs in the Negro League.

February 1945: Maj Charity E.Adams and Capt Abbie N.Campbell (in raincoat) inspect the first unit of African American WACs – 6888th Postal Directory Bn – to serve in the United Kingdom. All ranks wear the four-pocket service coat, with garrison caps apparently piped in the original WAC branch colors of mixed green and old gold. Note that they all seem to wear ankle socks over their stockings, and field shoes. (NARA)

Lieutenant Robinson is depicted wearing the M1943 field jacket in OD shade No.7, over a khaki shirt and light shade OD tie. When the service coat was not worn – as here – a single officers' cutout national cypher and arm-of-service insignia were to be pinned to the right and left shirt collar respectively.

D: INFANTRY, 1944–45

D1: Private first class, 555th Parachute Infantry Battalion (Colored); Camp Mackall, NC, spring 1945

A paratrooper of the only African American airborne unit, posing proudly in dress uniform after earning his "silver wings" – displayed on his left chest. He wears the garrison cap with light blue infantry piping, and on the left front the combined parachute-glider patch introduced in 1943. (This position could also be used to display enameled regimental badges, but they were seldom seen.) As prized as paratrooper insignia was the authorization to wear the pants bloused into highly polished "Corcoran" jump boots.

D2: First lieutenant Vernon J.Baker, 370th Infantry Regiment (Colored), 92nd Infantry Division; Viareggio, Italy, April 1945

Lieutenant Baker is depicted in field uniform of M1 helmet with camouflage net, shirt with rank and infantry insignia, M1943 field jacket with 92nd Division "Buffalo" insignia, and M1943 trousers. He carries the .30cal M1 carbine with two-magazine butt pouch, and the M1936 pistol belt supports a .45cal pistol in its russet leather M1916 holster, a two-magazine pistol ammo pouch and first aid pouch.

Vernon Baker was a platoon leader in the 370th Infantry; on April 5 and 6, 1945, in mountainous terrain near Viareggio, he crawled forward and destroyed three German machine-gun nests and an observation post, killing or wounding a dozen of the enemy. He then covered the evacuation of his company's casualties by occupying an exposed position and drawing the enemy's fire. Initially Baker was awarded the Distinguished Service Cross, the Army's second highest award for valor; but in 1997 his and similar decorations to six other African American soldiers were retrospectively upgraded to the Medal of Honor. Vernon Baker was the only one of the seven soldiers still alive to receive his award.

D3: Private, 370th Infantry Regiment, 92nd Infantry Division; Naples, Italy, August 1944

A soldier of the first combat unit of the division to disembark in Italy, wearing summer field uniform of helmet, light OD wool shirt with divisional sleeve insignia, OD wool pants, canvas leggings and field shoes (note that privates did not receive rank insignia until 1968). He is armed with the Garand M1 .30cal semi-automatic rifle, and wears full web gear on the march: M1923 rifle belt, canteen in M1917 cover, and M1928 haversack with integral suspenders, meatcan pouch and M1910 T-handle "intrenching tool."

E: SUPPORT & SERVICE TROOPS

E1: Chaplain

Each infantry regiment had three chaplains in its table of organization, and African American chaplains had a harder task than their white counterparts. Since they often had to intervene on behalf of their congregants in cases of maltreatment, they did more than simply care for their morale and spiritual wellbeing. With the status but not the authority

December 21, 1944: Lt(jg) Harriet Ida Pickens and Ens Frances Wills became the first African American women to be commissioned in the US Navy's WAVES – Women Accepted for Volunteer Emergency Service. (NARA)

of an officer, this chaplain wears the "pinks and greens" uniform with a service dress cap; his insignia include the rank bars of captain, and the Christian chaplain's silver cross on the lower lapels.

E2: Technician 3rd Grade, 92nd Quartermaster Company (Colored)

The Tech 3 was equivalent to a staff sergeant for pay purposes, but his grade indicated technical expertise rather than the command authority of "hard stripe" rank. Many African Americans found themselves in units of the Quartermaster Corps, responsible for supplies – a vital but underappreciated specialty. Many QM Cos, like this one, were numbered after the division to which they were assigned; they consisted of a headquarters, three transport platoons and one service platoon. This GI wears standard M1943 field uniform with insignia of grade and division.

E3: Technician 5th Grade, 152nd Coast Artillery Group (Colored)

Wearing the earlier "Parsons" field jacket with wool pants and leggings, this soldier – earning the pay of a corporal – belongs to a branch of service which saw many redesignations and changes of mission in the latter part of the war. In June 1944 the 54th Coast Artillery Regiment was redesignated 152nd Coast Arty Gp, under XXI Corps – whose shoulder sleeve insignia is illustrated here. However, only a month later the 152nd was disbanded and its men posted away to reinforce other coast artillery units.

F: SUPPORT & SERVICE TROOPS

F1: Master sergeant, 6888th Postal Directory Battalion (Colored), Women's Army Corps; UK, 1945

The WACs were a new branch of the US Army, formed in May 1942 in order to relieve men of clerical responsibilities and free them for more physical roles. The original concept had been to recruit 25,000 highly educated, middle-class white women to a Women's Army Auxiliary Corps (WAAC); fully incorporated into the armed forces as the Women's Army Corps (WAC) from July 1943, by the end of the war the Corps numbered nearly 100,000 – including just over 4,000 African American women – fulfilling more than 240 specific roles. This senior NCO is a member of the only African American WAC unit to see overseas service before VE-day. By this date the original and unpopular stiff, visored "Hobby hat" had given place to a garrison cap (by now made without the branch-of-service color piping). The M1944 wool field jacket, based on the British battledress blouse, was also a popular alternative to the four-pocket service coat for any who could get one. It was not officially authorized for servicewomen before VE-Day, but many in the ETO acquired locally approved examples made in Britain or France.

F2: Technician 4th Grade, Corps of Engineers; Italy, 1945

Though enjoying the pay grade of a sergeant, this Engineer technician probably has no special training in construction or engineering skills. Many African Americans were assigned to Engineer General Service units, which functioned as stevedores to unload supplies at ports in Europe and the Pacific.

F3: Sergeant, Military Police, 92nd Infantry Division; Italy, 1945

MP platoons – part of a division's HQ & HQ Company –
were larger than the term implies, with (by this date) 4 officers and 102 enlisted men, many of them NCOs, in a headquarters and two large sections each the size of a conventional platoon. African American MPs found themselves in a dilemma if confronted by white GIs, and tended to turn a blind eye to their misdemeanours while concentrating on men of their own units. Technically they had the right and authority to arrest any soldier breaking military law, but if he tried to arrest or even ticket a white soldier, the black MP might face an angry mob.

G: US NAVY & COAST GUARD

The Navy possessed a wide variety of uniforms designed for different uses. The enlisted "dungarees" or working uniform for "below decks" consisted of dark blue bell-bottom denim pants, a light blue cotton shirt and a white "dixie cup" sailors' cap. For wear "on deck" enlisted sailors had two different uniforms for summer and winter, but basically similar in design. Both featured a pullover "jumper" and bell-bottom trousers, in white and very dark blue respectively; the latter came in both dress and plainer working versions. The winter headgear, usually seen only in the USA or UK, was a flat-topped "Donald Duck" cap with a ribbon tally, but the white "dixie cup" was more usually worn even with the blues.

Navy officers also had a number of basic uniforms. The most common working dress in the Pacific consisted of a khaki shirt and trousers, worn with or without a black necktie, and either a khaki-topped service cap or a khaki garrison cap. The officers' summer dress uniform was a white single-breasted coat with a "choker" collar, matching trousers and a white service cap. Their winter dress uniform was a navy-blue double-breasted jacket with brass buttons, matching trousers and a blue-topped service cap, worn with a white shirt and black necktie. Chief petty officers wore a uniform of similar cut, with a service cap bearing simplified distinctions.

G1: Signalman 3rd Class, US Navy

The enlisted summer dress uniform is worn by this sailor, joining his ship and carrying his hammock. The white jumper has a plain matching flap collar worn with a black silk neckerchief; apart from his rating patch and the diagonal stripe indicating four years' service, both in black-on-white, it bears no insignia. Rating badges for the Seamen's branch were worn on the right sleeve, and by all other branches on the left; service stripes appeared only on the left forearm. The jumper is worn with white, pocketless trousers of only slightly bell-bottomed cut, and the white sailor cap.

G2: Storekeeper 2nd Class, US Coast Guard

The USCG wore uniforms almost identical to the USN; this is the enlisted winter blue dress uniform. For both services the blue jumper had three white trimming tapes on the cuffs and around the blue flap collar, which had a small white star in each corner. Again, the rating badge and service stripes are worn on the left sleeve, but in white and red on dark blue for the winter uniform. The trousers were more widely bell-bottomed for the blue uniform. The flat-topped cap bears the gold tally "US COAST GUARD."

G3: Chief Machinist's Mate, US Navy

This is his rating – his job; his rank is chief petty officer, and as such he is entitled to a "square rig" dress uniform of similar cut to that of his officers. In peacetime it would take most of a 20-year Navy career to reach this rank, but this CPO has benefited from rapid wartime expansion of the service. The chief's navy-blue double-breasted jacket had two rows of four buttons (instead of an officer's two rows of three), and rating badges and service stripes were displayed on the sleeve as by junior ranks. The service cap had a black leather chinstrap, and the chief's fouled anchor badge on blue backing on the front of the crown.

H: US MARINE CORPS

The Marine full dress uniform consisted of a navy-blue, single-breasted, brass-buttoned coat with a "choker" collar, trimmed with red piping; a white belt, sky-blue trousers, and a white service cap. The winter service ("Alpha") uniform was in the Corps' distinctive forest-green: a four-pocket, open-neck coat with cloth belt, matching trousers, and service cap or garrison cap in the same color. The summer "Bravo" uniform consisted of a khaki shirt, necktie, trousers and garrison cap. The Marine "utility" uniform was made of greenish-drab herringbone twill and was designed to be worn in combat. It was worn with "boondockers" – rough-side-out brown leather boots similar in height to the Army service shoe.

H1: Gunnery Sergeant Gilbert H.Johnson; Montford Point Camp, NC, spring 1945

The career of the legendary "Hashmark" Johnson, senior drill instructor at Montford Point, is outlined in the body text. Here he is depicted in his forest-green winter service uniform; the garrison cap and both upper lapels bear the blackened USMC eagle-globe-and-anchor badge. The service coat has blackened buttons, and rank and service sleeve insignia in green-on-scarlet. His medal ribbons reflect his previous hitches in the US Army and US Navy before transferring to the Corps in 1942; below them he wears the Expert Rifleman shooting medal.

H2: Sergeant, "utilities"

This NCO, drilling at Montford Point, has his sleeve rank badge, and the Corps cypher and badge on the single left chest pocket, stenciled in black on his herringbone twill working and field clothing – the "utility uniform, HBT, sage green, P1941." The matching short-visored utility cap, with its gathered crown, also has the USMC badge stencil. For this everyday duty the trousers hang loose over the "boondockers," and no web equipment ("782 gear") is worn.

H3: Private first class, full dress uniform

"Dress blues" were not an issue or required purchase item for Marines during wartime, but many African Americans still bought this uniform in order to demonstrate their pride in their branch of service. The buttons and the Corps badges on the service cap and collars are bright gilt, and rank insignia gold-on-red; hidden at this angle are the three-button cuff flaps, trimmed at top, rear and bottom with red piping. The sky-blue trousers had red "blood stripes" only for NCOs and officers. The cap peak, chinstrap and boots were polished dark brown "Cordovan" leather. When worn with a frame-buckle Cordovan garrison belt, instead of this white dress belt with a brass plate, this was termed "undress" uniform.

OPPOSITE
Capt Della H.Raney, US Army Nurse Corps, led the nursing staff at the post hospital at Camp Beale, CA; she was the first African American nurse in the US Army during World War II. (NARA)

BELOW
April 1943: a platoon of African American USMC recruits at Montford Point Camp, NC, are addressed by their drill instructor, Sgt Gilbert H. "Hashmark" Johnson – see Plate H1. (NARA)

INDEX